Hands-On Game Development Patterns with Unity 2019

Create engaging games by using industry-standard design patterns with C#

David Baron

BIRMINGHAM - MUMBAI

Hands-On Game Development Patterns with Unity 2019

Acquisition Editor: Karan Gupta
Content Development Editor: Keagan Carneiro
Technical Editor: Rutuja Vaze
Copy Editor: Safis Editing
Project Coordinator: Pragati Shukla
Proofreader: Safis Editing
Indexer: Priyanka Dhadke
Graphics: Alishon Mendonsa
Production Coordinator: Jyoti Chauhan

First published: March 2019

Production reference: 1280319

Published by Packt Publishing Ltd.
Livery Place
35 Livery Street
Birmingham
B3 2PB, UK.

ISBN 978-1-78934-933-7

www.packtpub.com

`mapt.io`

Mapt is an online digital library that gives you full access to over 5,000 books and videos, as well as industry leading tools to help you plan your personal development and advance your career. For more information, please visit our website.

Why subscribe?

- Spend less time learning and more time coding with practical eBooks and Videos from over 4,000 industry professionals

- Improve your learning with Skill Plans built especially for you

- Get a free eBook or video every month

- Mapt is fully searchable

- Copy and paste, print, and bookmark content

Packt.com

Did you know that Packt offers eBook versions of every book published, with PDF and ePub files available? You can upgrade to the eBook version at `www.packt.com` and as a print book customer, you are entitled to a discount on the eBook copy. Get in touch with us at `customercare@packtpub.com` for more details.

At `www.packt.com`, you can also read a collection of free technical articles, sign up for a range of free newsletters, and receive exclusive discounts and offers on Packt books and eBooks.

Contributors

About the author

David Baron is a game developer with over 15 years' experience in the industry. He has worked for some of the top AAA, mobile, and indie game studios in Montreal, Canada. He has a skillset that includes programming, design, and 3D art.

As a programmer, he has worked on a multitude of games for various platforms, including virtual reality, mobile, and consoles.

About the reviewers

Guillaume Leroy spent 20 years in the French Gendarmerie, including 10 years as an intelligence analyst and an economic defence advisor. After this, Guillaume retrained as a video game programmer in Montreal. Two years after starting his studies, he started his new career as a Unity generalist programmer at Playmind, where he is in charge of programming location-based games. Active in the local developer community, he leverages his network of contacts to further develop his skills and help others do so too.

I would like to extend my deepest thanks to David for giving me his trust to help him make this book and to allow me to live this new experience.

Johannes Unterguggenberger is a university assistant at TU Wien's Rendering and Modeling Group, Institute of Visual Computing and Human-Centered Technology, where he is engaged in teaching and research in the area of computer graphics. He has gained experience with Unity in several commercial and private projects, which were mainly focused on the areas of mobile game development and augmented reality. Although he currently focuses primarily on low-level graphics development with C++, OpenGL, and Vulkan, Unity and C# will always be two of his favorite technologies and have a special place in his heart.

I would like to thank Packt Publishing for the opportunity to be technical reviewer for a second time. It is a great pleasure and an honor to contribute to high-quality literature in the fields of computer graphics and game development.

Packt is searching for authors like you

If you're interested in becoming an author for Packt, please visit `authors.packtpub.com` and apply today. We have worked with thousands of developers and tech professionals, just like you, to help them share their insight with the global tech community. You can make a general application, apply for a specific hot topic that we are recruiting an author for, or submit your own idea.

Table of Contents

Section 7: Optimization Patterns

Section 8: Anti-Patterns in Unity

Preface

First principles, Clarice: simplicity. Read Marcus Aurelius,

"Of each particular thing, ask: What is it in itself? What is its nature?"

~ Hannibal Lecter

The preceding quote from one of my favorite films sums up my approach to learning. Following over a decade working in the gaming industry, I have found that the only valid way to gain mastery over a complex system is by breaking it down into its most basic components. In other words, I try to understand the core ingredients before mastering the final form.

You will see that throughout this book, I'm taking a very simplistic approach in the way I present each pattern. The goal is not to dump down the subject matter, but learn by isolating the core concepts behind each design pattern so that we can observe them and learn their intricacies. I've learned this approach in the gaming industry while working as a designer and programmer. We will often build components and systems for our game in isolated levels that we call *gyms*. We would spend weeks iterating, testing, and adjusting each ingredient of our game individually until we understood how to make them work as a whole.

I wrote this book in a way that's consistent with how I approach game development so you, as a reader, can immerse yourself in the subject matter while taking some good habits along the way that will help you in your career.

Even if the code included in each chapter is not what we call *production-ready*, it still offers a good starting point to build robust systems for your game. Hence, it's important to keep in mind that the code in this book is not dogma, but learning material that is meant to be improved by you, the reader. And I hope you do so!

Who this book is for

This book was written for beginner and experienced Unity developers. But it was also designed to be a reference for developers who are switching to Unity from other development environments and who wish to know how they can apply design patterns while using the core features of Unity's API.

What this book covers

Chapter 1, *Unity Engine Architecture*, explains the core architectural pillars of the Unity game engine.

Chapter 2, *Game Loop and Update Method*, reviews two core design patterns that every game programmer needs to understand, the game loop and the update method.

Chapter 3, *Prototype*, implements a spawn system using the prototype pattern as its foundation.

Chapter 4, *The Factory Method*, covers the Factory pattern, a close cousin of the Abstract Factory. We will use it to design a spawn system to generate non-player characters.

Chapter 5, *Abstract Factory*, covers the core differences between the Abstract Factory and the Factory Method while building an advance spawn system.

Chapter 6, *Singleton*, reviews the infamous singleton pattern, probably the most widely-used design pattern in Unity.

Chapter 7, *Strategy*, covers the basics of the Strategy pattern and how to use it to implement a collection of target-seeking behaviors for a missile system.

Chapter 8, *Command*, reviews the command pattern and how to use it to build a universal control system to command remote devices.

Chapter 9, *Observer*, explains what the observer pattern is and examines how to use it correctly in Unity with C#.

Chapter 10, *State*, covers the basics of the state pattern and how to use it to implement finite states for a game that revolves around a spaceship.

Chapter 11, *Visitor*, covers the basic principles of the visitor pattern and how to use it to implement a simulation of a one-armed factory robot.

Chapter 12, *Façade*, uses the façade pattern to prototype a system that enables a player's progress in a game to be saved.

Chapter 13, *Adapter*, covers the basics of the adapter pattern and how to use it to adjust an online user management system without modifying its code.

Chapter 14, *Decorator*, reviews the basics of the decorator pattern and how to use it to prototype a weapon customization system.

Chapter 15, *Event Bus*, covers the basic principles of the event bus pattern and how to use it to implement a global event-driven messaging system.

Chapter 16, *Service Locator*, reviews the basics of the service locator pattern and how to use it to implement a system that allows the registration and location of specific services at runtime.

Chapter 17, *Dependency Injection*, studies the core concepts behind IoC containers and how they relate to DI. We will then see an example of a dependency issue prompted by the implementation of a feature that permits the customization of the initial configurations of a superbike for a racing game.

Chapter 18, *Object Pool*, reviews the basics of the object pool pattern and how to use it to optimize a spawn system for a zombie game.

Chapter 19, *Spatial Partition*, reviews the basic principles of the spatial partition pattern and how to use it to prototype a mini-game in which a predator hunts prey in an environment.

Chapter 20, *The Anti-Patterns*, reviews a list of common anti-patterns and how to avoid them.

To get the most out of this book

Some basic functional knowledge of Unity and C# is required in order to get the most from this book.

Download the example code files

You can download the example code files for this book from your account at www.packt.com. If you purchased this book elsewhere, you can visit www.packt.com/support and register to have the files emailed directly to you.

You can download the code files by following these steps:

1. Log in or register at www.packt.com.
2. Select the **SUPPORT** tab.
3. Click on **Code Downloads & Errata**.
4. Enter the name of the book in the **Search** box and follow the onscreen instructions.

Once the file is downloaded, please make sure that you unzip or extract the folder using the latest version of:

- WinRAR/7-Zip for Windows
- Zipeg/iZip/UnRarX for Mac
- 7-Zip/PeaZip for Linux

The code bundle for the book is also hosted on GitHub at `https://github.com/PacktPublishing/Hands-On-Game-Development-Patterns-with-Unity-2018`. In case there's an update to the code, it will be updated on the existing GitHub repository.

We also have other code bundles from our rich catalog of books and videos available at `https://github.com/PacktPublishing/`. Check them out!

Download the color images

We also provide a PDF file that has color images of the screenshots/diagrams used in this book. You can download it here: `https://www.packtpub.com/sites/default/files/downloads/9781789349337_ColorImages.pdf`.

Code in Action

Visit the following link to check out videos of the code being run:

`http://bit.ly/2Wty3SJ`

Conventions used

There are a number of text conventions used throughout this book.

`CodeInText`: Indicates code words in text, database table names, folder names, filenames, file extensions, pathnames, dummy URLs, user input, and Twitter handles. Here is an example: "You can see by the following code example how easy it is to implement a reference to a component of a GameObject and call its `public` methods."

A block of code is set as follows:

```
public class Tomahawk : Missile
{
    void Awake()
    {
        this.seekBehavior = new SeekWithGPS();
    }
}
```

Bold: Indicates a new term, an important word, or words that you see on screen. For example, words in menus or dialog boxes appear in the text like this. Here is an example: "Create two GameObjects with the **Drone** or **Sniper** scripts attached to them as components."

 Warnings or important notes appear like this.

 Tips and tricks appear like this.

Get in touch

Feedback from our readers is always welcome.

General feedback: If you have questions about any aspect of this book, mention the book title in the subject of your message and email us at customercare@packtpub.com.

Errata: Although we have taken every care to ensure the accuracy of our content, mistakes do happen. If you have found a mistake in this book, we would be grateful if you would report this to us. Please visit www.packt.com/submit-errata, selecting your book, clicking on the Errata Submission Form link, and entering the details.

Piracy: If you come across any illegal copies of our works in any form on the internet, we would be grateful if you would provide us with the location address or website name. Please contact us at copyright@packt.com with a link to the material.

If you are interested in becoming an author: If there is a topic that you have expertise in, and you are interested in either writing or contributing to a book, please visit `authors.packtpub.com`.

Reviews

Please leave a review. Once you have read and used this book, why not leave a review on the site that you purchased it from? Potential readers can then see and use your unbiased opinion to make purchase decisions, we at Packt can understand what you think about our products, and our authors can see your feedback on their book. Thank you!

For more information about Packt, please visit `packt.com`.

Section 1: The Fundamentals

The objective of this section is to give the reader an overview of Unity's architecture. The following chapter is included in this section:

- Chapter 1, *Unity Engine Architecture*

Unity Engine Architecture

1

We are about to start on a journey that will teach us how to use software design patterns inside the Unity engine's development environment. This book takes a very hands-on approach to learning and applying design patterns. We are going to avoid getting lost in academic definitions of patterns and instead focus on implementing them with Unity's API on genuine game-development use cases. For those that want to dig deeper into the theory of a specific pattern, at the end of each chapter, there will be references to further reading material.

But the most important note to keep in mind is that this book focuses on simplicity over complexity. That means the code examples and use cases are designed to be as simple as possible so we can concentrate on the essential elements of a pattern, while avoiding getting lost in complex implementations. As a reader, I encourage you to take the source code of each chapter, elaborate on it, and then make it your own.

However, before diving into a new game engine and start coding with its API, it's essential to understand its architecture. So, in this chapter, we will be reviewing the core engineering pillars of the Unity engine. But first, for those that are still new to game development, we are going to quickly discuss the core components that are common to most game engines and how they influence the way we write code for video games.

The following topics will be covered in this chapter:

- Engine architectures
- Unity's component system
- Unity's scripting API

Engine architectures

In this section, we will review the basic principles behind game engines. Of course, the focus of this book is not about mastering engine architecture. Nevertheless, it's wise to take the time to familiarize ourselves with an engine's core architecture before making a game with it. We don't want to be blindsided later on by technical details that will break our design choices.

What are game engines?

Game engines are what drives the game industry forward, and Unity is the best example of this. Since its release, the number of game studios has grown at an exponential rate. Unity has democratized the process of making video games by offering an extensible development environment for amateurs and professionals alike.

But for those unfamiliar with the concept of game engines, or even why they are called engines, I have a straightforward way to describe them. Look under the hood of your car, what do you see? Cables, filters, tubes, batteries, and gears connected but working in unison to run the vehicle. A game engine is very similar to the concept of a car engine, but instead of being made out of metal and rubber, it's pure software. If you look under the *hood*, known as the codebase of any modern game engine, you will see hundreds of systems, tools, and components all interconnected and running in unison.

So, if you are planning to produce a video game, the most critical decision you will have to make is what engine you are going to use, because this is what will be running your game. This single choice will influence every aspect of your production. Every department will be required to adjust and alter their pipelines and workflows. Many games have been canceled or have ended up being bug-ridden disasters because of an unwise choice in engine technology.

That's one of the reasons that Unity became so popular, as its name implies, it's an engine that has the core intention of unifying the game industry. You can find Unity being used to build games ranging from Angry Birds clones to epic **Japanese Role-playing Game (JRPGs)**; in other words, it's genre-agnostic. By combining all the best practices of the industry and integrating them into a unique but straightforward development environment, Unity has made its engine a cornerstone of the industry.

 Please note that Unity is a closed codebase. Only partners of Unity have direct access to the source code of the engine. So there's a certain degree of speculation when we talk about the inner workings of Unity's architecture. That's why we are keeping this chapter very high-level and not diving too deep into specifications.

Unity's architecture

Now it's time to tackle our main subject, Unity and its core engine architecture pillars. One thing we must keep in mind is that Unity is a closed source engine; this means that we have to extrapolate our mental model of its overall architecture from its official documentation. To avoid going into gray areas of Unity's design that cannot easily be validated, we will focus on the most visible and useful pillars for us to know. The two main core engine architecture pillars are as follows:

- Components
- Scripting API

Components

Unity is a component-driven engine, and it's with a combination of components that we build our game. If we analyze the following graph, we can see there's a high-level hierarchy that entities contain other entities. The essential elements of this structure are the Components; they are the building blocks of a game:

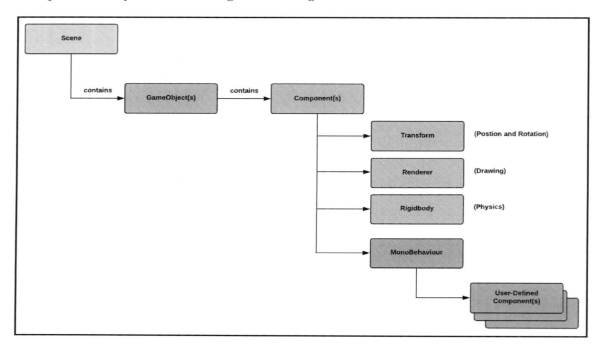

A simple way to visualize this architecture is to consider that a **Scene** is a collection of GameObjects, and GameObjects are a collection of Components that can implement and include the following:

- Systems (cameras and physics)
- Data (configurations, animations, and textures)
- Behaviors (game mechanics and scripted events)

So with this approach, we can quickly transform a GameObject that's behaving like a camera into an animated character by merely changing the components that it holds. That means that GameObjects are *composed* of components, and, depending on what type of component we attach to a GameObject, it will *morph* it into a specific kind of entity such as a camera, animated character, or particle. So it's a very straightforward and modular approach to constructing a game.

In the next section, we will review the API that Unity provides, which permits us to write those various components.

Scripting API

The original designers of Unity understood if they wanted to make an engine that could be used by developers of various skill levels, they needed to design a programming environment that was easy to use, but flexible enough to make any types of game. They achieved this by wrapping and exposing the engine's core functionalities and libraries through a managed scripting API. So, this means that a Unity developer can focus on writing code without worrying about the intricacies of memory management, or the inner workings of the engine.

This approach is common even with AAA in-house engines. The core components of the engine are usually coded in low-level programming languages, like C++ and assembly language because you need precise control over memory and processing usage. But programmers that are responsible for implementing in-game systems, such as AI behaviors or gameplay mechanics, can code on a higher layer of the engine's architecture. So engine programmers will often expose an API or library for gameplay programmers, so they can implement in-game components in a safe and controlled environment.

Gameplay programmers will often implement another layer of abstraction in the form of a simple scripting language, such as LUA, so designers can script behaviors without having to know how to code. Some engines go even further with this approach of simplification by implementing a visual scripting environment; an excellent example of this is Unreal's Blueprint system.

The end goal of all these layers of abstraction is to make the process of building a game more accessible to developers of diverse expertise, but also protect the engine from crashing because of poorly-implemented code. In other words, we want to avoid having a designer crash the engine because he wrote a script that spawns a thousand enemy characters at once in a scene, and as a consequence, causes an insufficient memory exception. So, we want to make sure the API or scripting library, which we offer to those that create content with our engine, can assist them in avoiding provoking critical errors that might affect the overall stability of the development environment.

The following diagram showcases the architectural hierarchy and the chain of responsibility of a typical AAA game development team. As we go up in the chain, technical details become abstracted, and there's a higher level of focus on content creation:

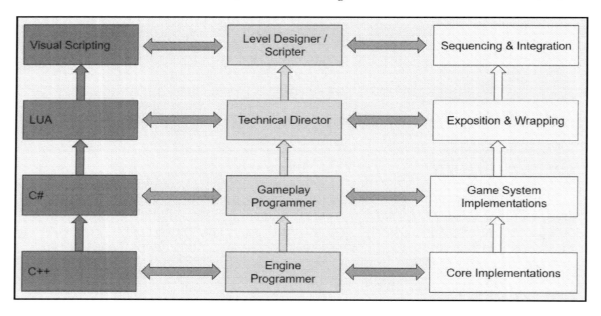

The purpose of this is to control access to the engine's limited resources, while exposing core features to the end user, which are usually designers and artists. And so, Unity's Scripting API has a similar purpose; its objective is to expose Unity's core features to the end user, in this case, developers, while protecting the inner workings of the engine.

So, the combination of a scripting API and a component system gives us a very simple, but powerful, coding model in Unity. You can see by the following code example how easy it is to implement a reference to a component of a GameObject and call its `public` methods:

```csharp
using UnityEngine;

public class PlayerCharacter : MonoBehaviour
{
    public float m_Range = 10.0f;
    public float m_Damage = 12.0f;

    private Weapon m_Weapon;
    private Inventory m_Inventory;

    void Awake()
    {
        m_Weapon = GetComponent<Weapon>();
        m_Inventory = GetComponent<Inventory>();
    }

    void Start ()
    {
        m_Inventory.Loadout("default");
    }

    void Update()
    {
        if (Input.GetKeyDown(KeyCode.UpArrow))
        {
            m_Inventory.EquipNextWeapon();
        }

        if (Input.GetKeyDown(KeyCode.Return))
        {
            m_Weapon.Shoot(m_Range, m_Damage);
        }
    }
}
```

This approach to programming games is straightforward, but also powerful. In this book, we are going to exploit the flexibility of Unity's API and its component driven architecture, while applying classic and modern software design patterns to make our code more robust. Our final goal is to build a toolkit of patterns that are adapted to Unity's unique coding model so we can develop games with a robust architecture.

For every industry-standard pattern or best practice, there's potential corresponding anti-patterns or drawbacks. It's important as a programmer to keep in mind not just the benefits of implementing a pattern, but also its potential pitfalls if incorrectly integrated into your overall architecture.

Summary

In this chapter, we started to explore the world of game engines and two of Unity's core engineering pillars:

- The component system
- The scripting API

Engines are very complex pieces of software, Unity has hundreds of features that we won't be able to cover in this book, but if we focus on mastering Unity's API, we will know how to access them when needs be.

In the upcoming chapters, we will focus on architecture, but more specifically, design patterns. We will learn how we can adapt proven industry patterns and best practices into Unity's unique coding model, without falling into the pitfalls of over-engineering. In the next chapter, we will review the two most critical concepts and patterns in game programming, the Game Loop and the Update method, which can be considered the heartbeat and ears of a video game.

Further reading

- *Game Engine Architecture* by Jason Gregory:
  `http://www.gameenginebook.com`

Section 2: Sequencing Patterns

2

In this section, we will review sequencing patterns, which are quite unique to game development. Unity's MonoBehaviour `Update()` magic method is a perfect example of the implementation of a sequencing method. The following chapter is included in this section:

- Chapter 2, *Game Loop and Update Method*

Game Loop and Update Method

2

In this chapter, we are going to explore the Game Loop and Update Method. Both are core game development patterns that are often confused with each other by beginners because they both can be associated with the concept of continuous looping sequences. But, as we are going to see, the Game Loop and Update Method might be related, but have very distinct responsibilities and are implemented on different layers of Unity's architecture.

If we want to understand the core principles behind the Game Loop and Update Method, then we need to consider what video games are in their most basic forms. The best definition I have encountered is that video games are simulations composed of interactive virtual spaces filled with objects and animated entities, with distinct behaviors. These virtual spaces are drawn frame by frame on a screen, while the continually-running system listens and reacts accordingly to a user's input.

But what exactly makes it possible for a video game to continually run a simulation and react to a user's input without any latency? The answer is the combination of the Game Loop, which can be described as the heartbeat of a running game, but also the Update Method, which can act as the ears of the system.

But as a Unity developer, you will never have to write a Game Loop or Update Method by hand, because they are already natively implemented in the engine. So, in the following sections, we are just going to explore the theory behind these patterns, so that we are of their presence when we are working in Unity.

The following topic will be covered in this chapter:

- A quick review of the core concepts behind the Game Loop and Update Method patterns

Technical requirements

In this chapter, we will focus on theory instead of practice; a basic understanding of programming is enough for this material.

What makes a game run?

As stated before, video games are simulations; a bullet buzzing through the air and then hitting an enemy combatant in *Call of Duty* is made possible because of a collection of systems interacting together to give the illusion that a 3D cylinder-shaped mesh traveling through space on a curved vector is being affected by gravity and wind resistance.

But the question we need to answer is, what is driving all these systems to run in perfect synchronization? Contrary to a spreadsheet or a browser, a video game is not event-driven; it's continuously processing, even when the player is not pressing any buttons. By implementing the Game Loop pattern, it's possible to have a system that cycles on itself at a constant rate, while calling sub-systems in perfect synchronicity, but still being able to react dynamically to a user's input.

So, in this section, we will review two core concepts: the implementation of the main loop, and the importance of timing, because the primary purpose of the Game Loop is to simulate time, not just execute code over and over again.

 You might notice that game designers often talk about core game loops. They are usually referring to what we call experience or reward loops. This subject is beyond the scope of this book, but we could say that games are composed of loops at almost every level.

The main loop

Even during the early 1980s, when programmers wrote games in pure assembly language without the help of an engine such as Unity, the concept of Game Loops existed. During that time, the implementation of a Game Loop needed to be precise in its timing, because it had to synchronize correctly with the movement of a CRT's television electron gun, or the image on the screen would get distorted and the game would become unresponsive.

The following is an example of a game loop written in assembly for an Atari 2600. You can see the main routine calling a specific sequence of sub-routines cyclically. Each sub-routine runs at a particular phase of an analog television's screen drawing sequence. Between every step, you can do calculations, capture the player's input, or draw sprites:

```
Main:
    jsr VSync ; Beginning of frame
    jsr VBlank ; Wait for electron gun to line up
    jsr Draw ; Draw sprites, UI and background
    jsr OverScan ; Ending frame
    jmp Loop ; Loop again
```

The modern day implementations of a game loop are not that different, they might be more sophisticated, but the core principles and sequencing pattern are similar. Every game loop must gather the player's input data and calculate new transforms on the entities in the scene before calling the rendering pipeline (also known as the draw loop). You can't draw something before knowing where things are supposed to be related to the most recent input of the player.

In this section, we reviewed that one of the primary responsibilities of the Game Loop is to make sure that subroutines are called in the right order at every cycle. In other words, it's maintaining a continuous sequence of system calls. But in the next section, we are going to review another important responsibility of the Game Loop, which is keeping a degree of consistent timing.

 Always keep in mind that a Game Loop and the Update Method are related, but they're not the same. They're both sequential patterns, but are not implemented the same way, and don't have the same responsibilities.

It's all about timing

As with comedy, timing is key to game programming; complex physics calculations are executed while thousands of pixels are rendered on a screen in a matter of milliseconds. Being aware of what is being called at every frame is key to mastering optimization.

In an engine such as Unity, the core game loop and rendering pipeline are abstracted, and we can only hook into its sequencing mechanism by the Scripting API's magic functions, such as: `FixedUpdate()`, `Update()`, and `LateUpdate()`. This approach permits the engine to protect its internal clock and its established sequence of system calls, while giving us the ability to execute code at specific moments of the Game Loop safely.

But the trade-off is that we lose granular control over the exact moment a specific system is updated. In most cases, this is not an issue, but for massive AAA production, this limitation can be a deal-breaker. Often, complex CPU-intensive games need a more granular approach to managing the timing of precise calculations; when having a ticking mechanism, this becomes essential. Instead of relying on trying to synchronize with the CPU's internal clock, Game Loops have a ticking mechanism that's very similar to what an analog watch might have. Like a clock, the Game Loop doesn't cycle around, but ticks. The Game Loop manages the variation of time between these ticks instead, depending on available operating systems and hardware resources. This approach permits us to have a more granular control in the way we schedule the processing time of specific game systems between every frame.

In the game industry, the terms *frame* and *tick* are often used interchangeably, but be careful, because they're not necessarily synonyms. We could say a **frame** is a unit of time based on the delay it takes to generate and draw a new frame onto the screen. And a **tick** is a unit of time that's related to a game's internal clock, which is simulated by the execution of the main game loop; it's similar to an analog clock's second hand ticks as it goes around the clock.

In the previous sections, we examined a very high-level and simplified overview of the Game Loop pattern. Of course, the actual implementation details of a Game Loop in a modern AAA game engine is beyond the scope of this book. For those that want to dive deep into the subject matter, and have a more academic understanding of the subject matter, I recommend reading the listed books in the *Further reading* section.

In the next section, we are going to explore Unity's implementation of the Update method.

Update Method

If we all agree that the Game Loop pattern's main goal is to abstract a CPU's clock cycle by implementing a ticker so we can time the execution of our code on every frame, in a consistent manner, then we could say that the Update Method pattern simplifies this process by offering a way to encapsulate our game entities, and let them update themselves on each frame.

In the following section of this book, we are going to review the Update Method and its implementation inside the Unity engine.

Over the years, I've noticed that game programming consists mostly of manipulating data with perfect timing. So, knowing how to manage data, and time, is essential for mastery of game programming.

Overview

One of the biggest challenges of implementing a Game Loop is keeping track of all the entities contained inside a scene, and how to update their states at every frame. But the Update Method offers a scalable, but straightforward solution, by having every object expose an Update() function that's called every frame.

The Game Loop is not aware of the content of the Update() function of each object, just that every object that has one should be called at every frame. So, we are basically encapsulating the updating process of each game object's state through a single interface.

Challenge

As we can see in the following example, a basic Game Loop implementation looks simple, but can be very complicated to implement correctly:

```
while (true)
{
    Capture();   // Listen and process the player's input.
    Update();    // Update the scene entity's positions and states.
    Render();    // Draw the frame.
}
```

Once we capture the player's controller inputs, we must update the transforms and states of our game's objects before drawing them on the screen. But to achieve this, we need to know what entities to update, and how to request them to do so. If these entities don't have a common object type or interface, we will need to manage them on a case-by-case basis:

```
Update()
{
    sceneEntities = scene.getEntities();

    for each entity in sceneEntities
    {
```

```
switch (entity.type)
{
    case Player:
    MovePlayer()
    break;
    case Camera:
    MoveCamera()
    break;

    // This switch case will get long.
    // Let's find a better way to do this.
    . . . . . . . . .
}
}
```

But our problems don't stop there; we also need to maintain a dynamic list of entities that will hold each object during their entire lifespan. As we can see, this type of approach doesn't scale well for larger games. So, the best solution would be to let the entities update themselves at every frame. In other words, let's have them encapsulate their behaviors, and the easiest to way to remind them to update themselves is to have a standard public function that we can call at every frame.

Let's see in the next section how we can resolve all these issues with the Update Method.

Solution

Now that we have found a solution that offers a standard interface to our game's scene entities and encapsulates them, we still need to maintain a list. Games are dynamic software; entities explode and spawn in a matter of seconds, manually managing a list of objects is error-prone.

But, if we had a common type for all our game's objects, then it will be easy for us to dynamically maintain a list of entities, and walk through it at every frame. If we have a container that holds all our game's objects, such as a scene, then we could iterate through it to find all the objects of a specific type, and call their Update() method.

That's mostly what MonoBehaviour is in Unity; it offers a common parent type for objects that are in a scene that need to update themselves at every frame. So, any component that is a child of the MonoBehaviour parent class has a magic method named Update(), which is called at every frame. So, while Unity does all the heavy lifting under the hood, you can focus on implementing the behaviors that you want to *tick* (update) at every frame by writing them inside a script's Update() method.

In the next section, we will dive deeper into Unity's implementation of the Update Method.

Unity's Update Method

As a Unity developer, we don't need to implement our Update Method; it's native to the engine's scripting API. But the Unity engineers expanded on the core concept and exposed several types of Update() methods; each one permits us to execute code at different moments in the period of a frame.

The following diagram is an example of the steps of execution during the time it takes to render a frame to the screen:

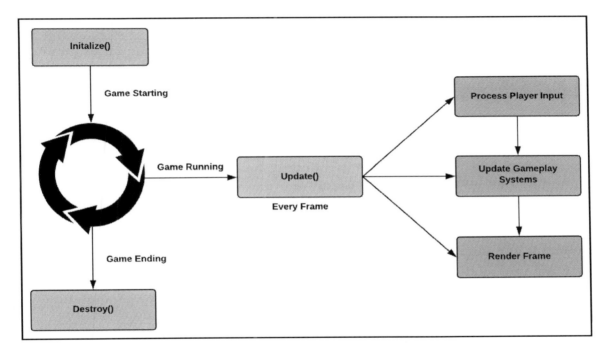

Each step in the diagram is completed in less than 1/30 of a second and in a constant order. But the Unity engineers had the foresight to know that having a singular Update() is not enough, because specific systems need to be processed in different moments of a frame. So they decided to expose three main types of Update() methods, which we'll review individually.

Take note that only objects that are active in a scene and that inherit from the MonoBehaviour parent class will have their various Update() methods called:

- **Update()**: This method is called on at the same frequency as the game's frame rate, which might be inconsistent, but at least frequent. In it, you should only implement code that needs to be executed in correspondence with every rendered frame. Because of its higher call frequency, it's a good place to implement your input listeners.
- **LateUpdate()**: This method is called after Update(). It's for code that needs to be executed after the completion of a call to Update(). Useful for camera movement translations that are dependent on the movement of a character that is being controlled by the player.
- **FixedUpdate()**: This method is called each time the physics simulation is ticked (updated). The timing of the calls of the FixedUpdate() method offers stable delta times between each frame. This approach is necessary for physics calculations and the simulation of certain types of behaviors, such as accelerated motion.
  The following segment showcases the intervals between an Update() and a FixedUpdate():

```
U = Update()

F = FixedUpdate()


-----U------U---U-----U----U----> Time
-----F-----F-----F-----F-----F---->
```

As we can see, a FixedUpdate() call is consistent, while an Update() varies over time.

The following is what the various Update Methods look like inside a typical MonoBehaviour script:

```
void FixedUpdate ()
{

}

void Update ()
{
```

```
}

void LateUpdate ()
{

}
```

The most important takeaway is that we always need to be aware of when our code will be executed. Unity simplifies this task for us by abstracting the inner ticking (updating) mechanisms of the engine and exposing it through the API in the form of various Update Methods.

Summary

In this chapter, we reviewed the Game Loop pattern and its core principles. Like many modern engines, Unity abstracts the inner working of its core game loop, instead of some API hooks, which permits us to control the timing of the execution of our code at each frame, without having to synchronize manually with the CPU's internal clock.

We also skated over the surface of the core concepts that encompass the Update Method pattern. As Unity programmers, we don't need to manually implement this pattern because it's native to the scripting API, but we still have to be aware of its purpose. A solid understanding of the timing and sequencing of Unity's update functions is essential. Even if we don't know what's happening under the hood, we can at least have control over the sequence of execution of our code.

In the next chapter, we will dive into practical design patterns and apply them to resolve real-life game architecture issues and challenges. Our first subject will be the *Prototype* pattern.

Further reading

- *Game Engine Architecture* by Jason Gregory:
  http://www.gameenginebook.com
- *Racing the Beam* by Nick Montfort and Ian Bogost:
  https://mitpress.mit.edu/books/racing-beam

Section 3: Creational Patterns

3

In this section, we will learn about Creational patterns by prototyping a grid-based spawning system for a dungeon crawling game. The concept of spawning is well-known: things appear in a game—sometimes it's particles, characters, or even the infamous loot boxes. In other words, as game developers, we need to make things pop up on the screen as fast as possible without slowing down the frame rate. There are some design patterns that might help in doing this. The following chapters are included in this section:

- Chapter 3, *Prototype*
- Chapter 4, *The Factory Method*
- Chapter 5, *Abstract Factory*
- Chapter 6, *Singleton*

3
Prototype

The goal of using the Prototype pattern is to assist in establishing a consistent way of making a copy of an object, based on a Prototype. This Prototype is usually an **archetypal object** that we need to create several times during the lifespan of our application. To avoid the potential performance costs of initializing new objects, we can use the Prototype pattern to set up a system that's very similar to a photocopying machine. By implementing the Prototype pattern, we will be able to make copies of archetypal objects on the fly while minimizing the impact on the overall performance of our application. In other words, the Prototype pattern is a handy tool to add to our programming toolbox.

The following topics will be covered in this chapter:

- We will review the Prototype pattern's core concepts.
- We will implement a spawn system, using the Prototype pattern as our foundation.

Technical requirements

This chapter is a hands-on chapter; you will need to have a basic understanding of Unity and C#.

We will be using the following specific Unity engine and C# language concepts:

- Interfaces
- Composition

If you are unfamiliar with these concepts, please review them before starting this chapter.

The code files of this chapter can be found on GitHub:

`https://github.com/PacktPublishing/Hands-On-Game-Development-Patterns-with-Unity-2018`

Check out the following video to see the code in action:

`http://bit.ly/2WviTwe`

An overview of the Prototype pattern

The Prototype pattern is categorized as a **creational pattern**, meaning that its primary responsibility is to optimize the process of initializing objects. In the Unity scripting API, we usually don't use constructors; instead, we convert our classes to components and attach them to GameObjects. With this approach, the engine manages the initialization sequence of our objects into the memory.

In theory, the initialization overhead of objects is out of our control, because the engine manages this for us. This statement is true to a certain degree, but it doesn't take into account what happens during the lifespan of a scene. If we need to load a prefab dynamically during a specific moment in a scene, the engine will not be able to prevent a sudden drop in the framerate as it loads the entire entity into the memory.

 A **prefab** is a prefabricated container of a collection of assembled GameObjects and components. For example, you can have a prefab for each type of character in your game. Prefabs are easy to load and copy into memory. They are often referred to as the building blocks of a game.

The Prototype pattern offers a simple solution to this technical hurdle; instead of loading up a new prefab, we copy one that's already in the memory. Similar to a photocopying machine, we can make any number of copies that we need from a single reference. This approach is valid for spawning both prefabs and individual components.

The following UML diagram is an example of a design for a spawn system that uses the Prototype pattern as a foundation:

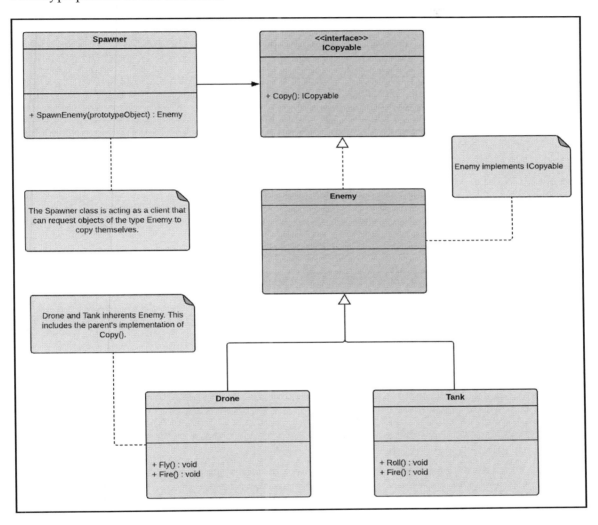

As you can see, the core element of the Prototype pattern is the interface class named `ICopyable`. As its name suggests, any class that implements `ICopyable` will need to be able to return a copy of itself. In the preceding diagram, the `Enemy` class implements the `ICopyable` interface. This relationship indicates that we will be able to request instances of **Drone** and **Tank** without having to create new ones every time.

> Associating a design pattern to a real-world system can help you to remember the definition of a specific pattern. Personally, I always compare the Prototype pattern to a photocopier.

Benefits and drawbacks

Let's review a short list of the benefits and potential drawbacks related to the implementation of the Prototype pattern.

The following are the benefits:

- **Reduction of initialization overhead**: In theory, copying an object that's already in the memory is faster than initializing a new one.
- **Reusability of instances in the memory**: It's possible to copy permutations of a prototype object while it is transferring from one state to another.
- **Consistency**: There are structural benefits to letting objects copy themselves; it's safer, and it offers a standard interface for the duplication process.

The following are the drawbacks:

- **Maintenance of references**: If there's a race condition in which we always destroy our prototype object before making a copy of it, we will end up nullifying any benefits of using this pattern.
- **Unsupported and circular references**: In some instances, objects have internal structures that don't support cloning. In those cases, it might be difficult to use the objects in a system that implements the Prototype pattern.

> In this book, we will avoid using strict computer science terminology. With any programming concept, there's always a scientific and practical definition. We will focus on the practical definitions while still considering the theoretical interpretations of the patterns.

Use case example

Now that you have a general understanding of the Prototype pattern, let's implement an actual in-game system, using the pattern as the foundation of our architecture. A spawn system is a perfect use case for a creational pattern like the Prototype pattern. Spawning enemies at the right moment is key to designing a very immersive experience in a video game.

The most critical technical issue that we need to avoid is a dip in the framerate during the spawning process of the enemies. That is why we are going to use the Prototype pattern; we will copy existing instances of specific enemies, instead of creating new ones each time we need to spawn them.

In the next section, we will take the UML diagram that we reviewed at the beginning of the chapter and implement it in actual code.

Code example

In this section, we will implement a bare-bones spawn system for a game that includes drones and snipers as its main enemy types. At this point, let's make sure that our spawn system can return copies of a specific enemy type to a client.

When we use the term **client** in this book, we mean a class that uses the functionality of a pattern. In our context, it's usually a `Client` class that permits us to test our code examples.

Throughout this book, we will often use interfaces in our examples. They're a powerful tool in object-oriented programming. They offer a simple way to declare an implementation contract. Refer to the following steps:

1. As our first step, let's implement an interface called `ICopyable`. We are going to expose a function called `Copy()`:

   ```
   public interface iCopyable
   {
       iCopyable Copy();
   }
   ```

   Notice that our interface is named `ICopyable`; this is to avoid confusing it with C#'s native interface, called `ICloneable`, which is used to declare a class as being **cloneable**. We are not going to use this C# interface in our example.

2. Now that we have our interface, let's implement it in a concrete class named Enemy:

```
using UnityEngine;

public class Enemy : MonoBehaviour, iCopyable
{
    public iCopyable Copy()
    {
        return Instantiate(this);
    }
}
```

Our Enemy parent class is now able to return a cloned instance of itself through the Copy() function. As we mentioned previously, we didn't use the C# native ICloneable interface because we are utilizing Unity's API by using its Instantiate() function. This API function is more suitable to our context because it can persist the hierarchical relationships of a native Unity GameObject or component during the cloning process. In other words, when cloning a GameObject with Instantiate(), you are copying (cloning) its children as well. This approach is essential in Unity because GameObjects are often composed of multiple objects and components, structured in a parent-child arrangement.

3. The next step involves implementing our two main enemies; let's start with Drone:

```
public class Drone: Enemy
{
    public void Fly()
    {
        // Implement flying functionality.
    }

    public void Fire()
    {
        // Implement laser fire functionality.
    }
}
```

As you can see, our Drone class is now a child of the Enemy class, and because child objects inherit the properties of their parents in object-oriented environments, the Drone class obtains access to the Copy() function. This arrangement means that a client will be able to request a copy of a Drone by calling Copy().

4. Now, let's do the same for our `Sniper`:

```
public class Sniper : Enemy
{
    public void Shoot()
    {
        // Implement shooting functionality.
    }
}
```

5. Now that we have all of our concrete `Enemy` type classes written down, let's implement our `EnemySpawner`:

```
using UnityEngine;

public class EnemySpawner : MonoBehaviour
{
    public iCopyable m_Copy;

    public Enemy SpawnEnemy(Enemy prototype)
    {
        m_Copy = prototype.Copy();
        return (Enemy)m_Copy;
    }
}
```

Our spawn system is quite simple; it spawns enemies by making copies of any object that he receives that corresponds to the `Enemy` type. It's like a Xerox machine; feed it the right document, and it will make copies of it. However, there's one core difference; our `EnemySpawner` doesn't do the copying. It just asks the object that it receives to make a copy of itself, and then returns the copy to the client.

6. To test our enemy spawn system implementation, let's write a `Client` class:

```
using UnityEngine;

public class Client : MonoBehaviour
{
    public Drone m_Drone;
    public Sniper m_Sniper;
    public EnemySpawner m_Spawner;

    private Enemy m_Spawn;
    private int m_IncrementorDrone = 0;
    private int m_IncrementorSniper = 0;
```

```
        public void Update()
        {
            if (Input.GetKeyDown(KeyCode.D))
            {
                m_Spawn = m_Spawner.SpawnEnemy(m_Drone);

                m_Spawn.name = "Drone_Clone_" + ++m_IncrementorDrone;
                m_Spawn.transform.Translate(Vector3.forward *
m_IncrementorDrone * 1.5f);
            }

            if (Input.GetKeyDown(KeyCode.S))
            {
                m_Spawn = m_Spawner.SpawnEnemy(m_Sniper);

                m_Spawn.name = "Sniper_Clone_" + ++m_IncrementorSniper;
                m_Spawn.transform.Translate(Vector3.forward *
m_IncrementorSniper * 1.5f);
            }
        }
    }
```

Our Client class is quite simple; depending on whether the player presses *S* or *D* on their keyboard, it will request EnemySpawner to return a Drone or Sniper instance, and then it will place it beside the previously spawned entity.

In this book, we assume that the reader has basic Unity skills and already knows how to set up GameObjects and attach components to them. As a quick reminder, to make this code example compile and work in a Unity scene, you will need to do the following:

1. Create two GameObjects with the **Drone** or **Sniper** scripts attached to them as components.
2. Create one GameObject with the **Client (Script)** attached to it.
3. In the **Inspector** of the **Client (Script)** component, set the **Drone** and **Sniper** GameObjects as references in the corresponding fields.

The following screenshot displays a typical Unity scene setup for testing our code example:

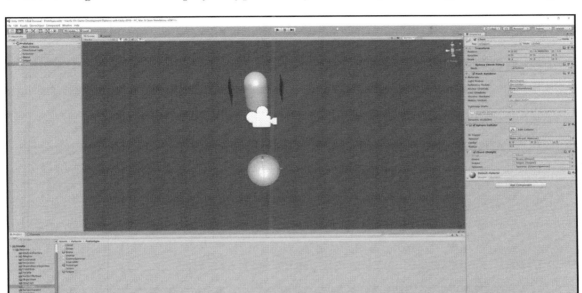

The source code and Unity project for this book are available in the GitHub repository at https://github.com/PacktPublishing/Hands-On-Game-Development-Patterns-with-Unity-2018.

We have successfully implemented the Prototype pattern while building a simple spawn system. This code is a solid foundation for developing a more advanced spawn system. The most important lesson to keep in mind is to always consider copying an object before creating it. This approach is a straightforward optimization strategy.

Summary

We started the practical section of this book with a flexible but simple pattern. The overall concept behind the Prototype pattern is straightforward; instead of initializing new objects, we merely clone them from instances that are already in the memory. To maintain consistency during the cloning process, we encapsulate the manner in which objects clone themselves, removing this responsibility from the client. As a benefit, we can gain performance and consistency in the way that we spawn entities in our game.

In the next chapter, we will explore the Prototype pattern's close cousin, the Factory pattern.

Exercise

Every time you learn a new pattern and adapt it to Unity, you should validate whether it is beneficial beyond making your code look structured. Unlike in other domains, game programmers are judged not just by their ability to write clean code, but also by how fast it runs. You will notice that a lot of design patterns sacrifice performance for consistency in structure.

As an exercise, I recommend that you compare the performance of using `Instantiate()` by copying an existing object in the memory to that of using `Resource.Load()` to load up an existing prefab of the same object.

To accomplish this task, you can experiment with Unity's native profiling tools.

 I recommend reading Unity's Profiler documentation; you can view the link in the *Further reading* section of this chapter. It's a good practice to profile your code often, especially before attempting any optimization. This approach will help you to avoid spending hours optimizing code that's not even executed that often.

Further reading

- *Game Programming Patterns* by Robert Nystrom: `http://gameprogrammingpatterns.com`
- *Unity Manual – Profiler overview:* `https://docs.unity3d.com/Manual/Profiler.html`

The Factory Method

4

The Factory Method is probably the most famous design pattern because it offers a solid structural base for most software architectures. There are two main variations of this pattern:

- The Factory Method
- Abstract factory

The main difference between both patterns is that the Factory Method is centered around a single Factory Method, while the Abstract Factory provides a way to encapsulate and group factories that have a familiar theme. These descriptions might sound abstract at the moment, but we will implement both of these variations in separate chapters so that we can better understand the core differences between each type of Factory pattern.

On a personal note, my only issue with the Factory pattern, in general, is that programmers tend to be irregular in the ways they implement it, and so sometimes consistency is lost because of personal style. But as we are going to see throughout this book, the most popular patterns tend to have significant alterations in the way they are implemented by professional programmers. We are going to try and take an approach that's always compatible with Unity's API and coding model.

The following topics will be covered in this chapter:

- An overview of the Factory Method
- Implementing a **non-player characters** (**NPC**) spawn system while using the Factory Method as the foundation of our architecture

 The core difference between the Factory and Prototype patterns is that the Factory pattern is useful when you want to delegate the creation process of objects, while the Prototype pattern is an optimal solution when creating new instances of objects is too costly.

Technical requirements

This chapter is hands on; you will need to have a basic understanding of Unity and C# to continue.

We will be using the following specific Unity engine and C# language concepts:

- Enums
- Composition

If you're unfamiliar with these concepts, please review them before starting this chapter.

The code files of this chapter can be found on GitHub:

`https://github.com/PacktPublishing/Hands-On-Game-Development-Patterns-with-Unity-2018`

Check out the following video to see the code in action:

`http://bit.ly/2WvN2vp`

An overview of the Factory Method

The Factory pattern is one of those patterns whose name is a good indication of its core purpose. There's a robust real-world correlation that can help us visualize its intent – imagine yourself ordering a new car at a dealership. During this process, does the dealer inform you of the manufacturing process of your new vehicle? The answer is probably no; usually, the dealer sends your order to the factory, and then they ship the requested final product back to you.

In other words, as the consumer of a product, you should focus on ordering and receiving, not manufacturing and distributing. And that's the primary goal of the Factory pattern; it simplifies the *order* process of specific types of objects by providing an interface that's abstract to the inner workings of the *manufacturing* process of the requested objects.

As we mentioned in the introduction, there are two main variations of the Factory, but in this chapter, we will review only the simplest form of this pattern, which is the Factory Method.

Let's start by reviewing a UML diagram of a use case that's using the Factory Method:

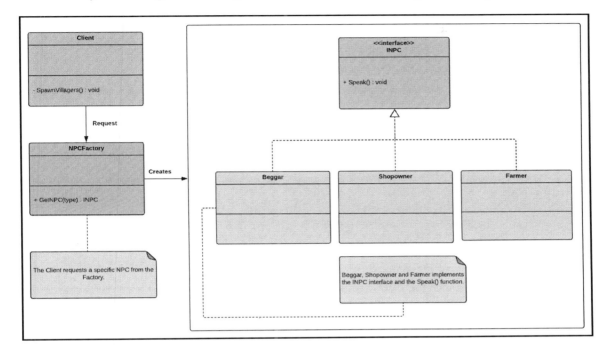

As we can see from this diagram, the `GetNPC()` method of the `NPCFactory` class is responsible for getting a specific type of NPC (**Beggar**, **Shopowner**, or **Farmer**). So, if a client requests a particular type of NPC, it needs to ask `NPCFactory` to produce it.

The core purpose of the Factory pattern is to abstract the creation and localize the creation process of a particular type of object.

Benefits and drawbacks

The Factory Method pattern has an excellent reputation and is often the cornerstone of a reliable code base. Let's have a look at a few of the benefits and drawbacks of the Factory Method.

These are the benefits:

- **Loose coupling**: Because the client doesn't need to know the details of the initialization process of a specific type of object, it reduces coupling and dependencies between classes
- **Encapsulation of the creation process**: The fact that the Factory Method takes the responsibility of creating specific object types, you can localize complex initialization processes in a single class

These are the drawbacks:

- **Extra code complexity**: Code becomes harder to read because you are adding abstraction and additional classes.
- **Open to interpretation**: Programmers often confuse the Factory Method and its cousin, the Abstract Factory. This issue might cause inconsistent implementations, which can provoke uncertainty and confusion between programmers working on the same code base.

 It's sometimes difficult to isolate recurrent drawbacks with a specific pattern because often it's a question of context. But a universal truth about design patterns is that they can become a regressive part of your architecture if you misapply them.

Use case example

Now that we have a basic understanding of the Factory Method, let's build a game system with it. To stay consistent with our previous chapter, we are going to implement another spawn system, but this time for NPCs. Because the Factory Method is a Creational pattern, it's a natural fit for a spawn system. As we are going to see in the following code example, the Factory Method is a perfect pattern to use when you need to centralize the initialization pipeline of various entities.

 In a professional game project, you might end up having to build separate spawn systems for different groups of entities. For example, in an open-world game, you might have a specific method to spawn civilians and one to generate cops because each primary type of AI character might have different requirements and loading processes.

Code example

As we mentioned before, the Factory Method is the most straightforward approach to implementing a Factory pattern. As its name implies, it primarily focuses on providing a standard interface for the creation of specific object types through a Factory Method. So, if we have a `Client` class that needs to initialize an object of a particular kind (also known as a **product**) but we don't know the exact class or the process to call, instead, we merely refer to a Factory to produce the requested product and return it to us. Let's follow these steps to get started with our example:

1. Let's build a simple spawn system for NPCs using the Factory Method as our base. But before we do that, we need to declare our general NPC type. The best way to do this in code is to have a standard interface for all our NPC characters. For reasons of simplicity, all of our NPCs entities will have a common functionality; they can speak scripted dialogue:

   ```
   public interface INPC
   {
       void Speak();
   }
   ```

2. Now that we have a standard interface for NPCs called `INPC`, we need concrete classes for each type of NPC that we might want to spawn. We will limit ourselves to the typical characters we might find in a farming village in a classical RPG game:

   - First is our `Beggar`, who begs for precious coins:

   ```
   using UnityEngine;

   public class Beggar : INPC
   {
       public void Speak()
       {
           Debug.Log("Do you have some change to spare?");
       }
   }
   ```

   - Then there's our `Shopowner`, who's always ready to sell us some goods:

   ```
   using UnityEngine;

   public class Shopowner : INPC
   {
       public void Speak()
   ```

```
    {
        Debug.Log("Do you wish to purchase something?");
    }
}
```

- Finally, we have our `Farmer`, with their words of wisdom:

```
using UnityEngine;

public class Farmer : INPC
{
    public void Speak()
    {
        Debug.Log("You reap what you sow!");
    }
}
```

3. So, now that we have concrete classes for each of our main NPC types, we need a way to refer to them when we need to. Let's write a public `enum` that will be easily accessible. We will disclose a list of available NPC types:

```
public enum NPCType
{
    Farmer,
    Beggar,
    Shopowner
}
```

4. The next step is to implement our `NPCFactory` class with a public Factory Method that will create the requested instance (product) of an NPC:

```
using UnityEngine;

public class NPCFactory : MonoBehaviour
{
    public INPC GetNPC(NPCType type)
    {
        switch (type)
        {
            case NPCType.Beggar:
                INPC beggar = new Beggar();
                return beggar;
            case NPCType.Farmer:
                INPC farmer = new Farmer();
                return farmer;
            case NPCType.Shopowner:
                INPC shopowner = new Shopowner();
                return shopowner;
```

```
        }
        return null;
    }
}
```

As we can see, our concrete implementation of the Factory Method is a function named GetNPC(), which is composed of a switch case that returns an INPC instance of a specified NPCType.

5. But the benefits of this design are evident in our client, which, in this example, will be our NPCSpawner class:

```
using UnityEngine;

public class NPCSpawner : MonoBehaviour
{
    public NPCFactory m_Factory;

    private INPC m_Farmer;
    private INPC m_Beggar;
    private INPC m_Shopowner;
    public void SpawnVillagers()
    {
        /**
        We don't want to specify the class to instiate for each
type
        of villager.
        Instead, we ask the factory to "manufacture" it for us.
        **/

        m_Beggar = m_Factory.GetNPC(NPCType.Beggar);
        m_Farmer = m_Factory.GetNPC(NPCType.Farmer);
        m_Shopowner = m_Factory.GetNPC(NPCType.Shopowner);

        m_Beggar.Speak();
        m_Farmer.Speak();
        m_Shopowner.Speak();
    }
}
```

6. We can test this implementation of the Factory Method and the NPCSpawner with the following test class:

```
using UnityEngine;

public class Client : MonoBehaviour
{
```

```
public NPCSpawner m_SpawnerNPC;

public void Update()
{
    if (Input.GetKeyDown(KeyCode.S))
    {
        m_SpawnerNPC.SpawnVillagers();
    }
}
}
```

We are now able to spawn instances of a specific NPC without having to know the location or the exact name of its concrete class. It might not look impressive when dealing with just three basic types, but imagine if every type of NPC had a different initializing process with multiple dependencies.

For example, imagine a circumstance in which the Beggar NPC is not a character but a behavior component that can be attached to any civilian character in our scene, while the Farmer NPC type is a self-contained prefab. With a Factory Method, we don't have to keep in mind all of these specifications every time we want to spawn a specific NPC; instead, we let the Factory Method do the dirty work for us and decide the best way to create those particular entities.

 Choosing between using an abstract or an interface when implementing a common parent for a specific family of objects can be daunting. In this example, I decided to go with an interface because I didn't want to share implementations – I wanted to declare a group type.

Summary

In this chapter, we were introduced to the core principles of the Factory pattern and implemented its first variation, the Factory Method. With this pattern, we can localize the creation process of types of objects. This might be fine and dandy, but what happens if we want complex products that combine various kinds of objects each with their specific creation method? Are we going to need to know and call each factory separately and assemble them manually?

This issue is what we are going to solve in the next chapter by implementing a more advanced version of the Factory pattern; the **Abstract Factory**.

When you analyze the usefulness of a design pattern, always keep in mind that they are designed for teamwork. The Factory is a perfect example of this. As a solo developer, you might find most design patterns redundant, but imagine yourself working on a massive code base with dozens of programmers. In that case, layers of abstractions and common interfaces can help you maintain your sanity as your team and code base grows.

Practice

In the previous chapter, we learned how to design a spawn system by using the Prototype pattern as our base. Due to this, our system behaved basically like a Xerox machine; it made copies of existing instances. This mechanism reduced the initialization overhead, but this was only beneficial if we already had a reference in memory to copy.

But now, we have the Factory Method in our toolkit; we can localize the process of creating new objects of certain types. What would be interesting to try is combining both. Could you have the Factory Method check if an instance of that type of object already exists in memory?

Combining patterns is a good exercise and will give you a broader range of approaches to complex implementations.

Further reading

- *Game Programming Patterns* by Robert Nystrom: `http://gameprogrammingpatterns.com`
- *Design Patterns: Elements of Reusable Object-Oriented Software* by Erich Gamma, John Vlissides, Ralph Johnson, and Richard Helm: `http://www.informit.com/store/design-patterns-elements-of-reusable-object-oriented-9780201633610`

5
Abstract Factory

In the previous chapter, we explored the Factory Method, a direct, straightforward, variation of the Factory pattern. Now, we will implement a more advanced version of the Factory pattern: the well-named Abstract Factory. The primary goal of both forms of the Factory pattern is to encapsulate the creation process of objects. In this chapter, we will focus on isolating the main differences between the Factory Method and Abstract Factory, so that we can better understand in which context we might choose one over the other.

The following topics will be covered in this chapter:

- The basics of Abstract Factory
- Designing an NPC spawner using the Abstract Factory pattern

 Explaining the core differences between the Factory Method and Abstract Factory is sometimes used as a trick question in technical interviews. So, having a clear answer to this type of question can impress your interviewers.

Technical requirements

This chapter is very hands-on, so you will need to have a basic understanding of Unity and C#.

We will be using the following Unity engine and C# language concept(s):

- Enums

If you are unfamiliar with these concept(s), please review them before starting this chapter.

The code files of this chapter can be found on GitHub:

https://github.com/PacktPublishing/Hands-On-Game-Development-Patterns-with-Unity-2018

Check out the following video to see the code in action:

`http://bit.ly/2HKybdy`

An overview of the Abstract Factory

The Abstract Factory is often explained in overly complicated terms in academic documentation, but if you distill it to its elementary form, its design and intent are quite simple. The main purpose of the Abstract Factory is to organize the manufacturing process of products (objects) into related groups. This approach allows us to manage factories that produce specific families of products (objects). In other words, we are able to add layers of abstraction to the creation process of particular categories of products (objects), and specific individual types.

In the following diagram, we can see the basic structure of the Abstract Factory described visually:

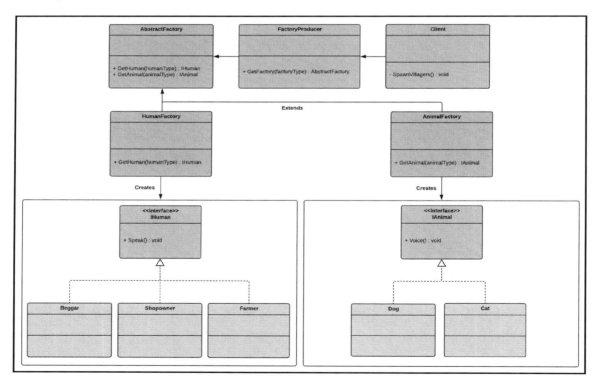

Notice the following members of this pattern:

- `FactoryProducer` is responsible for returning individual factories of a specific category (families) of products (Human or Animal)
- `HumanFactory` and `AnimalFactory` are responsible for the creation of Human or Animal products

The benefit of using Abstract Factory is obvious when you are dealing with the creation of a catalog of products, with each group having its unique manufacturing specifications.

 When describing a Factory pattern, we often use real-world terms such as *products*, *manufacturing*, and *producer*. It's always a wise approach to find correlations between real-life notions and computer science terms, because it helps in identifying and remembering their core purpose.

Benefits and drawbacks

The benefits and drawbacks of the Abstract Factory are very similar to those of the Factory Method, so it doesn't warrant repeating them in this chapter. But there's one significant benefit, which is the core difference between both patterns, that we need to address. While the Factory Method focuses on exposing a method that permits us to request the creation of objects of specific types, the Abstract Factory goes beyond this, by giving us a way to manage the creation of particular groups of objects.

This distinction might not sound important at first, but, if we consider a real-world analogy, such as the process of manufacturing a car, we can see why the Abstract Factory is advantageous. Your typical car is assembled with individually manufactured components, but the process of constructing an engine and tires is entirely different, so you need separate factories to create those crucial pieces of the final product. That's why the Abstract Factory is beneficial in software development, because it offers us a similar approach to structuring and organizing the way we produce a final, complex product, featuring multiple components with different object creation processes.

Use case example

We are going to extend the use case from the Chapter 4, The *Factory Method*, by adding a new type of spawnable NPC, called Animals. So, in our example, Humans and Animals are considered non-playable characters, but have separate manufacturing processes, so they will need individual factories. This type of requirement is easily implementable with the Abstract Factory.

Code example

Our code example is almost the same as the one that we completed in Chapter 4, *The Factory Method*. But we are going to add more depth to the system by including specific families of NPCs; in our case, Humans and Animals.

1. One key element of the Abstract Factory is that each family of products has an associated factory:

```
using UnityEngine;

public class FactoryProducer : MonoBehaviour
{
    public static AbstractFactory GetFactory(FactoryType factoryType)
    {
        switch (factoryType)
        {
            case FactoryType.Human:
                AbstractFactory humanFactory = new HumanFactory();
                return humanFactory;
            case FactoryType.Animal:
                AbstractFactory animalFactory = new AnimalFactory();
                return animalFactory;
        }
        return null;
    }
}
```

Notice that the class is implemented like a Factory Method, because we use a simple `switch` case to return the correct `Factory` to the client depending on the requested type.

2. Now, we need an `abstract` class to maintain consistency in the implementation of each product-specific `Factory`:

```
public abstract class AbstractFactory
{
    public abstract IHuman GetHuman(HumanType humanType);
    public abstract IAnimal GetAnimal(AnimalType animalType);
}
```

3. Next up is our first concrete product factory, `HumanFactory`:

```
public class HumanFactory : AbstractFactory
{
    public override IHuman GetHuman(HumanType humanType)
    {
        switch (humanType)
        {
            case HumanType.Beggar:
                IHuman beggar = new Beggar();
                return beggar;
            case HumanType.Farmer:
                IHuman farmer = new Farmer();
                return farmer;
            case HumanType.Shopowner:
                IHuman shopowner = new Shopowner();
                return shopowner;
        }
        return null;
    }
    public override IAnimal GetAnimal(AnimalType animalType)
    {
        return null;
    }
}
```

4. And now, `AnimalFactory`, which will produce cats and dogs:

```
public class AnimalFactory : AbstractFactory
{
    public override IAnimal GetAnimal(AnimalType animalType)
    {
        switch (animalType)
        {
            case AnimalType.Cat:
                IAnimal cat = new Cat();
                return cat;
            case AnimalType.Dog:
                IAnimal dog = new Dog();
```

```
                    return dog;
        }
        return null;
    }

    public override IHuman GetHuman(HumanType humanType)
    {
        return null;
    }
}
```

Notice that both classes implement each other's `GetAnimal()` or `GetHuman()` function, but return a `null`, depending on the context. This approach is in case a client refers to the wrong factory when requesting a specific type of NPC; instead of throwing an exception, it will receive a null.

5. Instead of using strings in our `switch`-type condition block, we are going to implement enums for each type of product we support, including the associated factories, as follows. This approach will avoid errors and maintain consistency:

- `FactoryType`:

```
public enum FactoryType
{
    Human,
    Animal
}
```

- `HumanType`:

```
public enum HumanType
{
    Farmer,
    Beggar,
    Shopowner
}
```

- `AnimalType`:

```
public enum AnimalType
{
    Dog,
    Cat
}
```

6. Our Animals don't speak, but our Humans do, so they can't share a standard interface. In that case, we are going to implement one for each type, as follows:

- `IHuman`:

```
public interface IHuman
{
    void Speak();
}
```

- `IAnimal`:

```
public interface IAnimal
{
    void Voice();
}
```

7. Now, we need to write each concrete class for all our human and animal NPCs, as follows:

- `Beggar`:

```
using UnityEngine;

public class Beggar : IHuman
{
    public void Speak()
    {
        Debug.Log("Beggar: Do you have some change to spare?");
    }
}
```

- `Farmer`:

```
using UnityEngine;

public class Farmer : IHuman
{
    public void Speak()
    {
        Debug.Log("Farmer: You reap what you sow!");
    }
}
```

- `Shopowner`:

```
using UnityEngine;
```

```
public class Shopowner : IHuman
{
    public void Speak()
    {
        Debug.Log("Shopowner: Do you wish to purchase something?");
    }
}
```

- Dog:

```
using UnityEngine;

public class Dog : IAnimal
{
    public void Voice()
    {
        Debug.Log("Dog: Woof!");
    }
}
```

- Cat:

```
public class Cat : IAnimal
{
    public void Voice()
    {
        Debug.Log("Cat: Meow!");
    }
}
```

8. Finally, we can extend our NPCSpawner class to support the spawning of Animal and Human NPCs:

```
public class NPCSpawner : MonoBehaviour
{
    private IAnimal m_Cat;
    private IAnimal m_Dog;

    private IHuman m_Farmer;
    private IHuman m_Beggar;
    private IHuman m_Shopowner;
    private AbstractFactory factory;

    public void SpawnAnimals()
    {
        factory = FactoryProducer.GetFactory(FactoryType.Animal);
        m_Cat = factory.GetAnimal(AnimalType.Cat);
        m_Dog = factory.GetAnimal(AnimalType.Dog);
```

```
        m_Cat.Voice();
        m_Dog.Voice();
    }
    public void SpawnHumans()
    {
        factory = FactoryProducer.GetFactory(FactoryType.Human);

        m_Beggar = factory.GetHuman(HumanType.Beggar);
        m_Farmer = factory.GetHuman(HumanType.Farmer);
        m_Shopowner = factory.GetHuman(HumanType.Shopowner);

        m_Beggar.Speak();
        m_Farmer.Speak();
        m_Shopowner.Speak();
    }
}
```

9. As proof of our concept, our `Client` class can request `Animal` and `Human` NPCs from our `Spawner` without having to know the process behind the creation of the final product:

```
public class Client : MonoBehaviour
{
    public NPCSpawner m_SpawnerNPC;

    public void Update()
    {
        if (Input.GetKeyDown(KeyCode.U))
        {
            m_SpawnerNPC.SpawnHumans();
        }

        if (Input.GetKeyDown(KeyCode.A))
        {
            m_SpawnerNPC.SpawnAnimals();
        }
    }
}
```

As you can see, the Abstract Factory gives us a lot more flexibility than its cousin, the Factory Method. We can now manage families of products, and add more layers of abstraction to manufacturing processes.

Summary

In this chapter, we learned about the Abstract Factory, a close cousin of the Factory Method. As its name implies, Abstract Factory permits us to add layers of abstraction to the manufacturing process of specific types of product (objects). This pattern is very beneficial when dealing with multiple families of products. The main drawback of Abstract Factory, compared to the Factory Method, is that it's more wordy and involved.

In the next chapter, we are going to explore what is arguably the most famous design pattern of them all: the Singleton.

 While learning about Factory patterns, you might notice that we are using several terms related to traditional manufacturing processes. The manufacturing and software industries are quite related. Best practices associated with managing factories inspired several core ideas behind DevOps and Kanban, which are now cornerstones of robust software development processes.

Practice exercise

At this point in the book, we have reviewed the two most popular forms of the Factory pattern: the Abstract Factory and the Factory Method. However, as an exercise, I would recommend expanding your knowledge of factories by implementing a third form, for example, the static Factory Method.

You can learn about the static Factory Method pattern in Joshua Bloch's classic book, *Effective Java*. More information can be found in the *Further reading* section.

Further reading

- *The Phoenix Project* by Kevin Behr, George Spafford, and Gene Kim
  https://itrevolution.com/book/the-phoenix-project
- *Effective Java* by Joshua Bloch
  https://www.pearson.com/us/higher-education/program/Bloch-Effective-Java-3rd-Edition/PGM1763855.html

6
Singleton

The Singleton is the most infamous pattern in the industry, but ironically, it's very popular with Unity developers. In consequence, it has become somewhat the duct tape of programmers, overused as a quick fix instead of a cornerstone of a robust architecture. There are many ways to implement a Singleton, from the simple but unsafe to the complicated but robust; we will go with the latter, because if we need to implement an unpopular pattern, let's do it in a way that won't backfire on us.

The following topics will be covered in this chapter:

- The basics of the Singleton's pattern
- Implementing the perfect Singleton in Unity

 Programmers love to argue, sometimes to the point of paralysis, so it's important never to become religious about design patterns. Always remember that there's no perfect solution; every design decision you make will have trade-offs.

Technical requirements

This is a hands-on chapter; you will need to have a basic understanding of Unity and C#.

We will be using the following specific Unity engine and C# language concept:

- Generics

If unfamiliar with this concept, please review them before starting this chapter.

The code files of this chapter can be found on GitHub:

https://github.com/PacktPublishing/Hands-On-Game-Development-Patterns-with-Unity-2018

Check out the following video to see the code in action:

`http://bit.ly/2YwBVEv`

An overview of the Singleton pattern

As its name implies, the Singleton pattern's main goal is to guarantee a singularity. This approach means if a class implements this pattern correctly, once initialized, it will have only one instance of itself in memory during runtime. This mechanism can be useful when you have a class that manages a system that needs to be globally accessible from a singular entry point.

As we can see from the following diagram, the Singleton's design is quite simple; unlike the Prototype pattern, a class implemented as a Singleton doesn't make a copy of itself but only returns its current instance to a client that's requesting it:

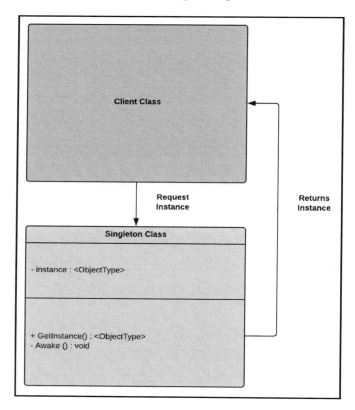

And if correctly implemented, a Singleton instance will even destroy any other instances of itself, just in case someone is trying to duplicate it. In other words, there can only be one. But we will see further in this chapter, implementing a solid Singleton in Unity is not as easy as it looks.

Benefits and drawbacks

The Singleton is a very controversial pattern; it's disliked by many because Unity developers frequently misuse it. If this contempt for this pattern is justified, I would say yes, but only to a certain degree. Instead of listing all the potential benefits and drawbacks of this pattern, I will present only one advantage and disadvantage; both are what I find to be the best arguments for or against the use of this pattern.

This is the benefit:

- **A singular point of entry**: The Singleton offers a singular but global access point to an instance of itself. This mechanism makes it easier to access dependencies that are exposed by a Singleton instance.

This is the drawback:

- **Obfuscation of dependencies**: Singletons are often used as *duct tape* to simplify access to complex interlocked dependencies. It's an easy solution that prevents the weeding out of wrong architecture choices.

So, taking into account these two arguments, there's a simple question we must ask when deciding to use a Singleton; is it because it's needed and fits with our overall architecture, or are we using it because it's a quick solution to a complex problem? From our answer, we can determine whether we are smart or just lazy with our design choices.

 When you are making design choices, it's important to always keep in mind whether your architecture is maintainable, scalable, and testable. If you can't individually test your modules, it's a good indication that your design has made your code base coupled and dependent on global dependencies.

Use case example

We must take into consideration that most games are made up of a collection of levels but each level includes a sequence of events during its lifespan, such as the following:

- Loading of previous save
- Triggering of introductory sequence
- Spawning of environment and characters
- Managing runtime game states
- Triggering the end scene sequence
- Save current player stats
- Trigger next level

To be able to manage this, we will need a Game Manager that will be active throughout the entire life span of a scene. As an analogy, if we look at the classic pen-and-paper version of Dungeons and Dragons, there's usually a Game Master that moderates and overlooks the flow of the game so the players can have a consistent but structured experience.

So, for our use case, we will need something similar but, of course, not as sophisticated as a human Game Master. The Singleton is a perfect pattern to implement a GM because it offers us a way to write a class as a singular but global entity that will accessible throughout the runtime of our game.

Code example

In this section, we will explore two versions of an implementation of the Singleton pattern in Unity. The first example is unsafe but straightforward. The second is advanced but more robust, as indicated at the beginning of this chapter.

Simple approach

Let's start by reviewing a simple way of implementing the Singleton in Unity. We have to keep in mind that we don't have access to a constructor when we use MonoBehaviours, so we will need to control the initialization of any member variables in the Awake() magic function, as follows:

```
using UnityEngine;

public class GameManager: MonoBehaviour
{
```

```
    public static GameManager instance;

    void Awake()
    {
        instance = this;
    }

    public void InitializeScene()
    {
        // Load persistent game state variables from the save system.
        // Load game systems and dependencies.
    }
}
```

As we can see, we have only one member, and it's static and public, which will make it easier for our clients to refer to it. In our `Awake()`, we pass our current `this` instance to the public static instance variable. This approach means our clients will have one constant and persistent access point to our `GameManager`, as seen in the following code snippet:

```
using UnityEngine;

public class Client: MonoBehaviour
{
    void Start()
    {
        GameManager.instance.InitializeScene();
    }
}
```

It looks pretty simple. We need to refer to the static instance member of the `GameManager` class, and we can call at any point its public functions. But there's one huge problem: this is not a Singleton for the reason that there's no mechanism in place that avoids having two instances of this object in memory.

We just implemented an interface to an instance of a global manager, but we are not protecting it from duplication in memory or preserving its integrity. Let's see whether we can do better with the next example:

```
using UnityEngine;

public class GameManager: MonoBehaviour
{
    public static GameManager _instance;

    void Awake()
    {
        if (_instance == null)
```

```
        {
            // Assigning only if there's no other instances in memory.
            _instance = this;
        }
        else if (_instance != null)
        {
            // Destroying itself if detects duplication.
            Destroy(gameObject)
        }
    }
}
```

Now, this is getting better. We are at least checking for `null` references before assigning the `_instance` static member, and avoiding potential duplicated instances of our `GameManager` by destroying them at the moment they *awake*.

This approach seems valid, but there's nothing that will guarantee consistency if you decide to have multiple classes implemented as Singletons. You might have one programmer writing a Singleton one way and another writing entirely differently. In the long run, this nullifies one of the fundamental benefits of design patterns; consistency in the architecture.

In the next section, we will look at a potential candidate for an advanced Singleton implementation that can become a pillar for our code base and offer us complete re-usability.

Advanced approach

The following class is an example of a complete Singleton implementation, but there's a lot to unpack here, so we are going to try to focus on the following essential elements:

```
using UnityEngine;

// <T> can be any type.
public class Singleton<T> : MonoBehaviour where T : Component
{
    // The instance is accessible only by the getter.
    private static T m_Instance;
    public static bool m_isQuitting;

    public static T Instance
    {
        get
        {
            if (m_Instance == null)
            {
```

```
            // Making sure that there's not other instances
            // of the same type in memory.
            m_Instance = FindObjectOfType<T>();

            if (m_Instance == null)
            {
                // Making sure that there's not other instances
                // of the same type in memory.
                GameObject obj = new GameObject();
                obj.name = typeof(T).Name;
                m_Instance = obj.AddComponent<T>();
            }
        }
        return m_Instance;
    }
}

// Virtual Awake() that can be overridden in a derived class.
public virtual void Awake()
{
    if (m_Instance == null)
    {
        // If null, this instance is now the Singleton instance
        // of the assigned type.
        m_Instance = this as T;

        // Making sure that my Singleton instance
        // will persist in memory across every scene.
        DontDestroyOnLoad(this.gameObject);
    }
    else
    {
        // Destroy current instance because it must be a duplicate.
        Destroy(gameObject);
    }
}
}
```

In this example, we are introducing **Generics**, a compelling C# feature that permits us to defer the type of a class at runtime. When we say a class is generic, it means that it doesn't have a defined object type. This approach is advantageous because we can assign it a specific type when we initialize it. In other words, it can become anything we want, and this could solve a core issue we are having with Singletons, which is the consistency of implementation between our classes that are Singletons.

Let's apply our generic Singleton class to a couple of Managers and see how we maintain uniformity in the way we write Singleton classes, as follows:

```
using UnityEngine;

// Inheriting Singleton and specifying the type.
public class GameManager : Singleton<GameManager>
{
    public void InitializeGame()
    {
        Debug.Log("Initializing the game.");
    }
}
```

As we can see, by inheriting the Singleton parent class, we have made our GameManager into a Singleton with one line of code (Singleton<GameManager>). This mechanism is possible because our parent class has all the core components of a Singleton.

Next up is another example of a Manager class converted into a Singleton with one simple line of code:

```
using UnityEngine;

// Inheriting the Singleton and specifying it's type.
public class InventoryManager : Singleton<InventoryManager>
{
    public void AddItem(int itemID)
    {
        Debug.Log("Adding item to the inventory.");
    }

    public void RemoveItem(int itemID)
    {
        Debug.Log("Removing item to the inventory.");
    }
}
```

We can test our new Singletons with the following Client class:

```
using UnityEngine;

public class Client : MonoBehaviour
{
    void Update()
    {
        if (Input.GetKeyDown(KeyCode.I))
        {
```

```
        GameManager.Instance.InitializeGame();
    }

    if (Input.GetKeyDown(KeyCode.A))
    {
        InventoryManager.Instance.AddItem(001);
    }

    if (Input.GetKeyDown(KeyCode.R))
    {
        InventoryManager.Instance.RemoveItem(023);
    }
}
}
```

Now that we have found a structured and reusable approach to the implementation of the Singleton pattern, we can safely integrate it into our code base while keeping in mind not to overuse it.

Summary

In this chapter, we tackled one of the most controversial design patterns out there. But we found a way to implement with a consistent and reusable approach. Even if the debate around the Singleton's usefulness persists, we can see how it can be beneficial for Unity developers.

We have completed the creational pattern section of the book, and now we have three core patterns in our toolkit, each with a specific function:

- The Prototype pattern offers us a way to create objects by copying them from a reference
- The Abstract pattern enforces the localization of the creation process of objects
- The Singleton offers a way to implement a mechanism that guarantees one singular instance of an object in memory

In the next chapter, we will transition out from Creational to Behavioral patterns. The first on our list is the Strategy pattern, a classic pattern that focuses on the dynamic selection of algorithms at runtime.

Exercise

The main issue with the Singleton pattern is that its instance is globally accessible and persistent, so if any component that has dependencies related to a Singleton object, it cannot be tested as an isolated unit. But in the real world, code bases are never perfect, and programmers often use Singletons.

So, you need to find a way to maintain proper unit testing best practices even when dealing with an architecture that is heavily dependent on global Singleton instances. So, as an exercise, I would recommend reading up on **test-driven development** (**TDD**) practices, especially core concepts such as **Stubs** and **Mocks**.

TDD is beyond the scope of this book, so please refer to the *Further reading* section for more information on the subject.

Further reading

- *Test Driven Development: By Example* by Kent Beck
  https://www.pearson.com/us/higher-education/program/Beck-Test-Driven-Development-By-Example/PGM206172.html
- *Real World: Test-Driven Development* by Mauricio Aniche
  https://www.goodreads.com/book/show/24400837-real-world-test-driven-development

Section 4: Behavioral Patterns

In this section, we will focus on how to best implement AI and UI systems and components using design patterns that focus on managing states and behaviors. With this knowledge, we will set up the basic building blocks to develop games of various genres, including **real-time strategy (RTS)**.

The following chapters are included in this section:

7
Strategy

Strategy is one of those patterns whose name doesn't indicate its intent explicitly. This uncertainty can make it hard to grasp and remember its purpose. But the Strategy pattern is quite simple: it offers a way to dynamically select algorithms and assign them to an object at runtime. We could imagine the Strategy pattern acting as a master chess player, analyzing the chessboard and choosing what strategy is best depending on the context.

The following topics will be covered in this chapter:

- The basics of the Strategy pattern
- Implementing a series of target-seeking behaviors for missiles using the Strategy pattern

Technical requirements

This chapter is a hands-on chapter, so you will need to have a basic understanding of Unity and C#.

We will be using the following specific Unity engine and C# language concept:

- Composition over inheritance

If unfamiliar with this concept, please review them before starting this chapter.

The code files of this chapter can be found on GitHub:

https://github.com/PacktPublishing/Hands-On-Game-Development-Patterns-with-Unity-2018

Check out the following video to see the code in action:

http://bit.ly/2UlVjVG

An overview of the Strategy pattern

The primary goal of the Strategy pattern is to defer the decision of which algorithm to use until runtime. This approach allows more flexibility and reusability of segments of code that implement logic and behaviors. This idea may sound very complicated, but it's a simple mechanism that's possible because of the object-oriented programming concept of *composition*. So, instead of sharing reusable algorithms by implementing them in a parent class that can be inherited by other classes, we instead wrap each algorithm into self-contained individual *components* that we attach to objects at runtime.

If this sounds familiar and resembles a lot how Unity's component system works, it's because the engine has what we call in object-oriented programming a *composition over inheritance* approach. So, this makes the Strategy pattern harmonious with Unity's architecture.

Let's review the following simple diagram of this pattern:

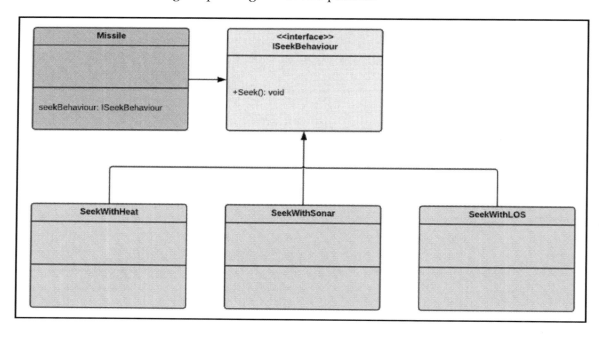

As we can see, this example of the Strategy pattern implements an interface that permits us to assign various seeking behaviors to any objects of the **Missile** type. But like most patterns, it can be tough to follow it's design just by looking at a UML diagram. Therefore, we can only truly understand the mechanism behind this pattern by implementing it in code, which we will see in the next sections.

 In this chapter, we will often use the terms algorithms, logic, and behaviors as synonyms because, in the context of the Strategy pattern, they are manageable as individual components.

Benefits and drawbacks

The Strategy pattern has a good reputation, but like most sophisticated patterns, its complexity can cause some drawbacks.

These are the benefits:

- **An alternative to subclassing**: Because it focuses on composition over inheritance, the Strategy offers a way to avoid hardwiring behaviors in each subclass of a parent type
- **Fewer condition statements to manage**: By implementing each behavior into individual components that can be managed by the Strategy pattern, the need for long conditional statements when dealing with complex contextual behavior selection is eliminated

Here are the drawbacks:

- **Client must be aware of the various strategies**: The Strategy pattern doesn't abstract itself from the client, so it must be aware of the different strategies and how to call them
- **Increased code complexity**: A common drawback of this type of sophisticated pattern is that it does increase the number of classes and objects to manage

 One of the main reasons that a lot of programmers hesitate to use sophisticated patterns is because they are afraid that junior members of the team might get lost in the complexity that it adds to a code base. So, it's important to diagram and document complex parts of your code and also list the patterns you are using to implement a system.

Use case example

For this use case, let's imagine we are working on a military simulation game and we are assigned to implement the following behaviors for the missile homing system:

- **Heat**: The missile seeks a target by its heat signature
- **Sonar**: The missile uses sound propagation to find a target
- **GPS**: The missile uses GPS coordinates to home onto the target

The design document also emphasizes that there will be three types of missiles using a homing system. But at the moment, it's not decided which missile will be using which homing system:

- **Tomahawk**: Usually launched from a carrier
- **SideWinder**: They are intended for jet fighters
- **Torpado**: They are designed to destroy underwater targets

So, now we have technical choices to make:

- Do we hard code each seeking behavior in the class of each type of missile?
- Do we write a single homing system class that will contain all the missile-seeking behaviors?
- Do we instead write each missile-seeking behavior as a separate component that we can attach dynamically to any missile?

The third option is the best one because it removes any duplicate code and offers flexibility in the form of composition. In the next section, we will implement this use case, and we will see how the Strategy pattern provides us a lot of extensibility.

Good code is flexible and never rigid. Rigidity might seem more stable, but it makes changes difficult and expensive.

Code example

We are going to keep this example very simple, so we can focus on understanding the Strategy pattern and not get lost in wordiness. Let's follow a step-by-step procedure:

1. Let's start by implementing the following critical element that makes this pattern work, which is the interface that will be used to access the seeking behaviors:

```
public interface ISeekBehaviour
{
    void Seek();
}
```

   Now that we have a standard interface for all our seeking behaviors, let's implements them in individual concrete classes.

2. Our first one is our `SeekWithGPS` behavior, as follows:

```
using UnityEngine;

public class SeekWithGPS : ISeekBehaviour
{
    public void Seek()
    {
        Debug.Log("Seeking target with GPS coordinates.");
    }
}
```

3. We have our `SeekWithHeat` behavior, as follows:

```
using UnityEngine;

public class SeekWithHeat : ISeekBehaviour
{
    public void Seek()
    {
        Debug.Log("Seeking target with heat signature.");
    }
}
```

4. Lastly, we have our `SeekWithSonar` behavior, as follows:

```
using UnityEngine;

public class SeekWithSonar : ISeekBehaviour
{
    public void Seek()
```

```
        {
            Debug.Log("Seeking with sonar.");
        }
    }
```

So, now that we have encapsulated each seeking behavior into individual classes, the next step is to find a way to assign them dynamically to missiles.

5. Let's write an abstract class that will group each type of missile with a common parent and permit us to give them a shared interface, as follows:

```
abstract public class Missile
{
    protected ISeekBehaviour seekBehavior;

    public void ApplySeek()
    {
        seekBehavior.Seek();
    }

    public void SetSeekBehavior(ISeekBehaviour seekType)
    {
        this.seekBehavior = seekType;
    }
}
```

There are two key things to notice: the `ApplySeek()` and `SetSeekBehaviour()` functions will apply a specified behavior to any missile type that derives from the `Missile` class. We have given ourselves a single point of access to all our missile types and a way to apply a seek behavior dynamically. Let's see how this looks in our concrete missile classes.

6. We are starting with our `Torpedo`. By default, let's give it the `SeekWithSonar` behavior, as follows:

```
public class Torpedo : Missile
{
    void Awake()
    {
        this.seekBehavior = new SeekWithSonar();
    }
}
```

7. Next up is our `SideWinder`. We should give it the `SeekWithHeat` behavior, as follows:

```
public class SideWinder : Missile
{
    void Awake()
    {
        this.seekBehavior = new SeekWithHeat();
    }
}
```

8. Our final missile type is going to be `Tomahawk`. Let's give it the `SeekWithGPS` behavior because it's a long-distance missile, as follows:

```
public class Tomahawk : Missile
{
 void Awake()
 {
 this.seekBehavior = new SeekWithGPS();
 }
}
```

We can notice that each concrete missile class assigns an instance of the seeking behavior to `this.seekBehaviour` at `Awake()`, and this is because we want to make sure each missile type has a default seeking behavior associated with it at initialization.

9. We will see in our `Client` class example that we can reassign a new behavior to a missile at any time we want, as follows:

```
using UnityEngine;

public class Client : MonoBehaviour
{
    void Update()
    {
        if (Input.GetKeyDown(KeyCode.D))
        {
            // Applying default seeking behaviour to missiles.
            Missile sideWinder =
ScriptableObject.CreateInstance<SideWinder>();
            sideWinder.ApplySeek();

            Missile tomahawk =
ScriptableObject.CreateInstance<Tomahawk>();
            tomahawk.ApplySeek();
```

```
                    Missile torpedo =
        ScriptableObject.CreateInstance<Torpedo>();
                    torpedo.ApplySeek();

                    // Applying custom seeking behaviour to a SideWinder.
                    Missile sideWinderWithSonar =
        ScriptableObject.CreateInstance<SideWinder>();
                    ISeekBehaviour sonar = new SeekWithSonar();
                    sideWinderWithSonar.SetSeekBehavior(sonar);
                    sideWinderWithSonar.ApplySeek();
                }
            }
        }
```

As we can see, we are now able to attach dynamically a seek behavior to any missile. This mechanism is beneficial because it means we could launch a missile and switch its seeking behavior mid-flight; a very cool feature to have in a game.

Summary

We have just learned how to implement the Strategy pattern by building a series of targeting seeking behaviors that can be attached to any missile at runtime. An important takeaway from this pattern is the importance of isolating behaviors into separate classes that can be assigned dynamically to objects. This approach has become a pillar of good architecture and very popular among game programmers.

In the next chapter, we will explore the command pattern, a behavioral pattern that is often used to manage the triggering of events.

Practice

In the preceding code example, we only implemented a simple prototype of missile targeting seeking behaviors to keep the chapter within a reasonable length and focus on learning the core concepts behind the Strategy pattern. However, it would be a great exercise to complete the implementation of those targeting behaviors and build a demo of a launching system that can dynamically switch a missile's homing system from a heat, sonar, or GPS seeking behavior.

Further reading

- Composition over inheritance:
  https://en.wikipedia.org/wiki/Composition_over_inheritance

8
Command

I have to admit that the Command pattern might be hard to understand at first. I know that it took me time to master it. Even if its name indicates its core purpose, its actual application is not apparent at first. But once you start playing around with it and comprehend its intricacies, it can become a sturdy pattern to apply when designing specific types of systems, such as user interfaces. Its primary purpose is to offer a way to encapsulate data that is needed to execute an operation or trigger an event at a particular moment.

The following topics will be covered in this chapter:

- The basic principles behind the Command pattern
- Implementing a Universal Controller that we can control multiple devices with

Technical requirements

The following chapter is hands on, so you will need to have a basic understanding of Unity and C#.

We will be using the following specific Unity engine and C# language concept:

- Constructors

If you are unfamiliar with this concept, please review it before moving forward.

The code files of this chapter can be found on GitHub:

`https://github.com/PacktPublishing/Hands-On-Game-Development-Patterns-with-Unity-2018`

Check out the following video to see the code in action:

`http://bit.ly/2Our6OF`

The basics of the Command pattern

The Command pattern is a solution that makes it possible to centralize the process of invoking specific commands on objects. A real-world correlation I keep in mind when thinking about the Command pattern is a *Universal Controller*. Back in the day, before the internet and smartphones, most living rooms had multiple devices, each with a specific functionality. You had a stereo to play music, a TV to watch shows, a VHS to play tapes, and so on, but each system had a particular remote control associated with it, so this often caused confusion because of the variety of controllers you needed to manage.

Due to this, the programmable *Universal Controller* was invented, which resolved this issue and allowed you to control multiple devices from a single remote. This approach worked because a *Universal Controller* had a standard set of buttons that you could associate with commands and devices.

In a way, the Command pattern is very similar to the concept of a *Universal Controller* because it permits you to link and invoke specific commands on objects that can handle requests.

Let's review the following diagram, which is of a typical implementation of the Command pattern:

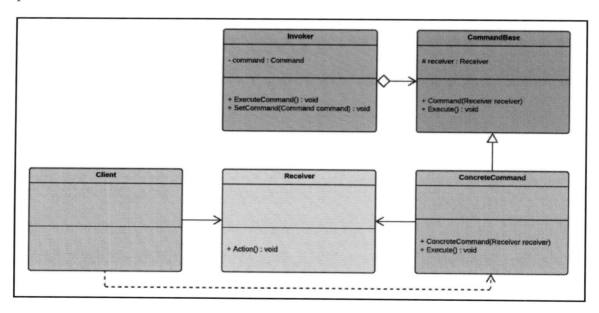

Trying to learn about the Command pattern by looking at a diagram is not the right approach, but it does help us isolate the fundamental classes that are participating in this pattern:

- An `Invoker` is an object that knows how to execute a command and can also do the bookkeeping of executed commands.
- The `Receiver` is a type of object that can receive commands and execute them.
- The `CommandBase` is usually an interface or abstract class for concrete command classes. It's the primary layer of abstraction of this pattern.

These core classes encapsulate all the information that's needed to execute a command at a specific moment. This will be made more evident when we implement our use case.

Benefits and drawbacks

Similar to patterns such as the Strategy and State, the main reason that programmers seem to avoid using the Command pattern is because of its *wordiness*.

These are the main benefits of the Command pattern:

- **Sequencing and timing**: The Command pattern gives you the flexibility of executing commands in a sequence or within a specific time frame
- **Undo/Redo**: The Command pattern is often used to implement bookkeeping features that permit to rollback commands in specific orders
- **Extensibility**: A typical advantage of Behavioral patterns is that they give you the ability to add behaviors with minimal changes having to be made to the main classes

These are the drawbacks of the Command pattern:

- **Verbosity**: A common disadvantage of this type of pattern is that it makes your code very verbose and adds a lot more classes to your code base

Use case example

As a use case, we will actually implement a Universal Controller that will permit us to control multiple devices, including a TV and radio. The main reason we are going to use the Universal Controller concept as an example is because it's going to be easier for us to learn the intricacies of the Command pattern, which we will do by implementing a system that is directly related to managing the invocation of commands on specific objects.

Code example

Implementing the Command pattern with a specific use case is the best way to master it. The example we are going to write is a perfect fit for the Command pattern because it's all about sending commands to specific receivers:

1. For our first class, we will need to declare the `RemoteControlDevice` type in the form of an abstract class:

```
abstract class RemoteControlDevice
{
    public abstract void TurnOn();
    public abstract void TurnOff();
}
```

2. Next up is the `Command` class, which is our core type for this pattern:

```
abstract class Command
{
    protected RemoteControlDevice m_Receiver;

    public Command(RemoteControlDevice receiver)
    {
        m_Receiver = receiver;
    }

    public abstract void Execute();
}
```

As we can see, its primary responsibility is to assign a `Receiver` object and `Execute()` a command.

3. Now, let's implement concrete Command classes, each with their unique responsibility. First off, let's implement `TurnOnCommand`, which is used to turn on our devices (receivers):

```
class TurnOnCommand : Command
{
    public TurnOnCommand(RemoteControlDevice receiver) :
base(receiver)
    {
    }

    public override void Execute()
    {
        m_Receiver.TurnOn();
    }
}
```

4. Next up is our `TurnOffCommand`, which will, of course, turn off our devices (receivers):

```
class TurnOffCommand : Command
{
    public TurnOffCommand(RemoteControlDevice receiver) :
base(receiver)
    {
    }

    public override void Execute()
    {
        m_Receiver.TurnOff();
    }
}
```

5. There's also our `KillSwitchCommand`, which is unique:

```
class KillSwitchCommand : Command
{
    private RemoteControlDevice[] m_Devices;
    private static RemoteControlDevice receiver;

    public KillSwitchCommand(RemoteControlDevice[] devices) :
base(receiver)
    {
        m_Devices = devices;
    }

    public override void Execute()
    {
```

```
            foreach (RemoteControlDevice device in m_Devices)
            {
                device.TurnOff();
            }
        }
    }
```

As we can see, `KillSwitchCommand` doesn't merely call the `Execute()` function on a `Receiver` object, but goes through a list of devices and calls the `TurnOff()` function on each of them. This means that we are batching the execution of a specific command.

6. Now we need to implement our devices that receive the orders to execute specific commands. Our first receiver is `Television`:

```
using UnityEngine;

class TelevisionReceiver : RemoteControlDevice
{
    public override void TurnOn()
    {
        Debug.Log("TV turned on.");
    }

    public override void TurnOff()
    {
        Debug.Log("TV turned off.");
    }
}
```

7. Our next receiver is `Radio`:

```
using UnityEngine;

class RadioReceiver : RemoteControlDevice
{
    public override void TurnOn()
    {
        Debug.Log("Radio is turned on.");
    }

    public override void TurnOff()
    {
        Debug.Log("Radio is turned off.");
    }
}
```

As we can see, both receivers have implemented the `TurnOn()` and `TurnOff()` functions. They are thus encapsulating the details of their unique behaviors.

8. Furthermore, let's implement a vital player of the `Command pattern`, `Invoker`:

```
class Invoker
{
    private Command m_Command;

    public void SetCommand(Command command)
    {
        m_Command = command;
    }

    public void ExecuteCommand()
    {
        m_Command.Execute();
    }
}
```

This example of `Invoker` is straightforward but can easily be extended to bookkeep the commands that are executed through it.

9. Finally, we have our `Client` class:

```
using UnityEngine;

public class Client : MonoBehaviour
{
    private RemoteControlDevice m_RadioReceiver;
    private RemoteControlDevice m_TelevisionReceiver;
    private RemoteControlDevice[] m_Devices = new
RemoteControlDevice[2];

    void Start()
    {
        m_RadioReceiver = new RadioReceiver();
        m_TelevisionReceiver = new TelevisionReceiver();

        m_Devices[0] = m_RadioReceiver;
        m_Devices[1] = m_TelevisionReceiver;
    }

    void Update()
    {
        if (Input.GetKeyDown(KeyCode.O))
        {
            Command commandTV = new TurnOnCommand(m_Devices[0]);
```

```
                    Command commandRadio = new TurnOnCommand(m_Devices[1]);
                    Invoker invoker = new Invoker();
                    invoker.SetCommand(commandTV);
                    invoker.ExecuteCommand();

                    invoker.SetCommand(commandRadio);
                    invoker.ExecuteCommand();
                }

            if (Input.GetKeyDown(KeyCode.K))
            {
                    Command commandKill = new KillSwitchCommand(m_Devices);
                    Invoker invoker = new Invoker();
                    invoker.SetCommand(commandKill);
                    invoker.ExecuteCommand();
                }
            }
        }
```

You will notice that there's a specific sequence of calls to be made when invoking a command:

1. Initialize a new Command
2. Pass it to `Invoker`
3. `Invoker` executes the specified Command

With this approach, we are maintaining a consistent channel of communication between those that invoke commands and those that receive them.

Summary

In this chapter, we reviewed the Command pattern, a unique pattern that tends to confuse a lot of programmers at first because its core usefulness is not always apparent. But once you apply it correctly, it does offer a lot of extensibility when implementing systems that are dependent on executing commands in specific orders on multiple components.

Next up is the Observer pattern, a pattern that's more easily understandable than Command and is the core of C#'s event system.

Practice exercise

The Command pattern is often used to implement the classic undo/redo functionality that you find in most text editors. In our code example, we implemented the groundwork to support this feature. So, as a practice exercise, I recommend that you integrate your own undo/redo feature. You can find cues on the best approach to this in the `Invoker` and `KillSwitchCommand` classes.

Further reading

- *Applying UML and Patterns,* by Craig Larman: http://www.craiglarman.com

9
Observer

In this chapter, we are going to learn about the Observer pattern, but we are going to take a different approach from our previous chapters, for the simple reason that the Observer pattern is already natively implemented in the Unity engine, in the form of the C# event system. But just to cover our bases, we will quickly review the classic form of the Observer pattern and then compare it to the C# event system.

The following topics will be covered in this chapter:

- The basics of the the Observer pattern
- Reviewing how it's implemented natively in the C# event system

Technical requirements

This is a hands-on chapter, so you will need to have a basic understanding of Unity and C#.

We will be using the following Unity-specific engine and C# language concept(s):

- Events
- Delegates
- Coroutines

You don't need to know about them before starting this chapter, but it would help to take the time to review some online documentation on the subject.

The code files of this chapter can be found on GitHub:

```
https://github.com/PacktPublishing/Hands-On-Game-Development-Patterns-with-
Unity-2018
```

Check out the following video to see the code in action:

```
http://bit.ly/2Fy4HvP
```

A preview of the Observer pattern

As its name implies, the purpose of the Observer pattern is to observe. To be more precise, the core purpose of the Observer is to observe other objects and specific changes in their internal states. Before the Observer pattern, the only way to watch an object from the *outside, looking in* was by calling constantly or *pinging* its public members in the hope that you would capture a change in its values.

The Observer pattern was designed to solve this limitation by defining a system in which objects (subjects) maintain a list of other objects (observers). Subjects call observers when they need to broadcast a change on their side.

We can visualize the principles of this system with this real-world example of a Wall Street broker managing a catalog of stocks (subjects) associated with a list of clients (observers). When particular market events occur, the broker calls all their clients to let them know that the value of their stocks has changed.

Let's review a UML diagram of a typical implementation of the Observer pattern to see how this might work when implemented in code:

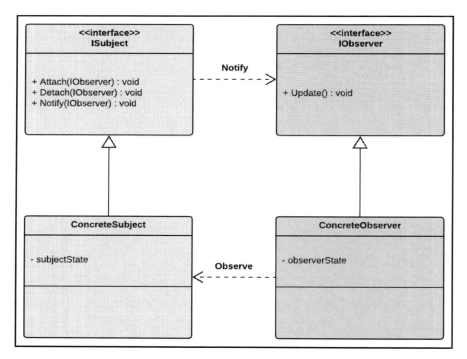

As you can see, the subject and the observer both have their respective interfaces, but the most important one to analyze is ISubject, which includes the following public functions:

- Attach(): This function allows the addition of an observer object to the list of observers to notify.
- Detach(): This one removes an observer from the list of observers.
- Notify(): This will notify all the observers that have been attached to the subject's observer list.

Even though this is not a very complicated design to implement, it can become very tedious to write each time you need to observe other objects. Modern languages such as C# have natively implemented the Observer pattern in the form of an event system, so programmers don't have to write it out manually.

 Unlike applications such as spreadsheets, which usually only change their current run-states depending on users' interactions, we must take note that games are not event-driven; instead, it's the main game loop that drives the game forward.

The C# event system

As a Unity developer, you will probably never need to implement a complete Observer pattern by hand because C# has a native implementation of the Observer natively available in the form of the event system. But before we start writing code, let's review the core components of the C# event system:

- **Events:** When an event is raised by an object (publisher), it sends out a signal that other objects (subscribers) can capture. This concept might sound very familiar to that of throwing and handling exceptions, in the sense that when an exception is thrown, it goes up the call stack until it's handled. But in the case of the event system, there's not really a call chain, because once an object broadcasts an event, only those objects that subscribe to it will be notified and can choose to get triggered by it or just ignore it. So, we can basically imagine it has as a sudden burst of a radio signal that only those with antennas can listen to.

- **Delegates:** The concept behind delegates is simple when you understand their underlying low-level mechanism. A high-level definition of delegates is that they hold references to functions. They are very useful when you want to trigger multiple functions from one call—in other words, when you want to multicast. But this is a very abstract definition of what delegates actually do behind the scenes. They're basically function pointers, which means that they hold the memory address to other functions. So, we could visualize them as an address book that contains a list of locations of functions. And that's why a delegate can hold multiple functions and call them all at once.

Benefits and drawbacks

The Observer is one of those patterns that has become embedded in modern languages and code bases. It would be hard not to use this pattern, as its drawbacks are limited.

The following is a list of the benefits:

- **Loose coupling**: The main advantage of the Observer is that it decouples observed objects from observers. They don't need to know one another; they just broadcast or listen.
- **Send data to anyone**: You can easily send data to and from one object to another.
- **Stop listening at any time**: There's no explicit contract between subjects and listeners, so they can stop broadcasting if needed.

The following is a drawback:

- **Noisy code**: The Observer pattern has brought about the event-driven paradigm, but it can can become noisy and difficult to manage, if overused

Use case example

The Observer pattern in the form of an event system is often used to manage user input, but let's see whether we can use events for something else, such as an automated system that broadcasts its state changes to other systems.

Let's say we are building a classic puzzle game with a countdown timer. As in most games or sports that have timers, we will give our player a unique sign and feedback to remind them how much time there is left.

Our three main timer feedback events are going to be as follows:

- Clock started
- Half time
- Time's up

For each event, let's trigger something unique, such as the following:

- Dim the lights
- Trigger a buzzer
- Display a message on the screen

But the challenge here is this: how are we going to notify the individual systems or components that manage the lighting, sounds, and UI of the state of the timer? When we have this type of problem, the Observer pattern becomes very useful, in the form of the event system: we will be able to have all those individual systems listen to the timer while it broadcasts specific timed events.

Code example

We are going to start this code example by implementing the most important component of an Observer pattern: the subject. Without something to observe, the Observer pattern has no use. Refer to the following steps:

1. In the case of our code example, the Timer class is going to be our subject:

```
using UnityEngine;
using System.Collections;

public class Timer : MonoBehaviour
{
    private float m_Duration = 10.0f;
    private float m_HalfTime;

    public delegate void TimerStarted();
    public static event TimerStarted OnTimerStarted;

    public delegate void HalfTime();
    public static event HalfTime OnHalfTime;

    public delegate void TimerEnded();
    public static event TimerEnded OnTimerEnded;

    private IEnumerator m_Coroutine;
```

```
IEnumerator Start()
{
    m_HalfTime = m_Duration / 2;

    if (OnTimerStarted != null)
    {
        OnTimerStarted();
    }

    yield return StartCoroutine(WaitAndPrint(1.0F));

    if (OnTimerEnded != null)
    {
        OnTimerEnded();
    }
}

private IEnumerator WaitAndPrint(float waitTime)
{
    while (Time.time < m_Duration)
    {
        yield return new WaitForSeconds(waitTime);

        Debug.Log("Seconds: " + Mathf.Round(Time.time));

        if (Mathf.Round(Time.time) == Mathf.Round(m_HalfTime))
        {
            if (OnHalfTime != null)
            {
                OnHalfTime();
            }
        }
    }
}
```

As you can see, there's not much code; it's quite simple to implement a subject with the C# event system. The most important thing is the relationship between the delegate and the event type. An *event* is a message sent by an object, but during the communication process, it doesn't know which objects will receive its message, so it needs a pointer-like mechanism that can act as an intermediate between the sender and the receivers, and that's when delegates are required. Just imagine the delegate as the one that points the event message to the right *observers*.

There's also another important detail to keep in mind. Notice that every time we call an event such as `OnTimerEnded()`, it checks for nulls on its associated event-type reference before raising the event:

```
....
if (OnTimerEnded != null)
{
    OnTimerEnded();
}
```

We do this because we can't broadcast an event if no one is listening. We need at least one observer that will handle the reception of the event. This is the way the event system is implemented and manages its references.

2. Now that we have our subject ready, it's time to implement the systems that will register themselves to receive event messages from our `Timer`. In other words, we are going to implement our observers. The first one is `Buzzer`, which will notify our player that the timer has started or ended, by making a buzzing sound:

```
using UnityEngine;

public class Buzzer : MonoBehaviour
{
    void OnEnable()
    {
        Timer.OnTimerStarted += PlayStartBuzzer;
        Timer.OnTimerEnded += PlayEndBuzzer;
    }

    void OnDisable()
    {
        Timer.OnTimerStarted -= PlayStartBuzzer;
        Timer.OnTimerEnded -= PlayEndBuzzer;
    }

    void PlayStartBuzzer()
    {
        Debug.Log("[BUZZER] : Play start buzzer!");
    }

    void PlayEndBuzzer()
    {
        Debug.Log("[BUZZER] : Play end buzzer!");
    }
}
```

3. The next one in our list is the `WarningLight`, which will blink when the timer reaches halftime:

```
using UnityEngine;

public class WarningLight : MonoBehaviour
{
    void OnEnable()
    {
        Timer.OnHalfTime += BlinkLight;
    }

    void OnDisable()
    {
        Timer.OnHalfTime -= BlinkLight;
    }

    void BlinkLight()
    {
        Debug.Log("[WARNING LIGHT] : It's half-time, blinking the
warning light!");
    }
}
```

4. As our final observer, we are going to implement `Notifier`, which has the responsibility of popping up a message when the time is up and the game is over:

```
using UnityEngine;

public class Notifier : MonoBehaviour
{
    void OnEnable()
    {
        Timer.OnTimerEnded += ShowGameOverPopUp;
    }

    void OnDisable()
    {
        Timer.OnTimerEnded -= ShowGameOverPopUp;
    }

    void ShowGameOverPopUp()
    {
        Debug.Log("[NOTIFIER] : Show game over pop up!");
    }
}
```

We should notice something that all our observers have in common: they all register themselves to receive events from the `Timer` by pointing to a specific local function. This implementation means that when the `Timer` broadcasts an event, all those objects that are observing it will get one of their local methods called automatically. Therefore, a remote event can provoke a local function call of an object:

```
// Adding the object as a observer of the OnTimerEnded event once it
//get's enabled.
void OnEnable()
{
    Timer.OnTimerEnded += ShowGameOverPopUp;
}

// In case the object is disabled, removing it as an observer of
//OnTimerEnded.
void OnDisable()
{
    Timer.OnTimerEnded -= ShowGameOverPopUp;
}
```

Another point to keep in mind is that an event can't point to `null` references, so it's good practice to make sure an object will remove itself as an observer if it gets disabled.

The Observer pattern expressed through the C# event system offers a simple but powerful way of implementing an observer-and-subject relationship between objects, without explicit coupling and with a few lines of code.

Summary

In this chapter, we have learned how to implement the Observer pattern by building a timer that can trigger behaviors in our scene by having components listen to specific timed events. An important take away from this pattern is that the Observer pattern is natively implemented in Unity in the form of the C# event system.

In the next chapter, we will explore the State pattern. Another useful pattern for game programming, it is somewhat related to the Observer pattern.

Exercise

As we have learned in this chapter, the Observer pattern was the inspiration for the C# event system. But, of course, it's not an exact implementation of this pattern. So, as an exercise, I would encourage you to re-write the timer system that we just implemented, but without using the C# event system; instead, follow the design of the Observer pattern.

You can use the UML diagram shown at the beginning of the chapter as a starting point.

It's common to see design patterns implemented in unorthodox ways. Often, design patterns inspire programmers to structure their code in a certain way, but rarely will you see an accurate and "by the book" implementation of a specific pattern in production code bases.

Further reading

Design Patterns, by Erich Gamma, Richard Helm, Ralph Johnson, and John Vlissides (http://www.pearsoned.co.uk/bookshop/detail.asp?WT.oss=design%20patterns%20elementsWT.oss_r=1item=171742)

10
State

In video games, objects continually transition from one state to another depending on events that might be triggered by the player or the game's mechanics.

So, one of the primary responsibilities of a game programmer is to implement a list of finite states and behaviors for entities, ranging from **non-player characters** (**NPCs**) to weapons. These tasks must be accomplished in a way that's maintainable and configurable so that a team of designers can tweak each stateful behavior individually until the game feels balanced.

The State pattern was designed precisely to accomplish this by offering a simple way to encapsulate behaviors into individual classes that represent the specific states of an object.

This chapter will cover the following topics:

- The basics of the State pattern
- Implementing a collection of finite states for a game involving a spaceship

Technical requirements

The following chapter is hands-on, so you will need to have a basic understanding of Unity and C#.

We will be using the following Unity-specific engine and C# language concept:

- Interfaces

If you are unfamiliar with this concept, please review it before moving forward with this chapter.

The code files of this chapter can be found on GitHub:

https://github.com/PacktPublishing/Hands-On-Game-Development-Patterns-with-Unity-2018

Check out the following video to see the code in action:

http://bit.ly/2UfzpTD

The basics of the State pattern

The State pattern is very similar to the Strategy pattern in the sense that it permits us to apply behaviors at runtime to a specific object. The core difference is that the State pattern is used when we need to manage an object's internal states, while the Strategy pattern focuses on choosing the right algorithm to execute, depending on the runtime context.

In the context of a class structure for a spaceship project, the following diagram shows how state classes (NormalShipState, AlertShipState, and DisabledShipState) have a standard interface that permits the Ship class to invoke the behavior of a specific state:

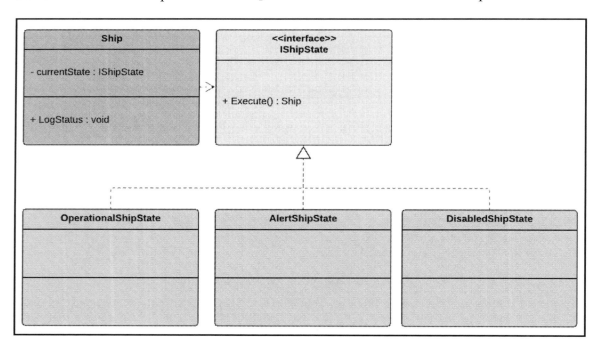

As we will see in the code example, the concept behind the State pattern is as simple as its actual implementation, because it offers us a way to encapsulate behaviors and apply them, without resorting to long conditional statements.

Benefits and drawbacks

It can be challenging to pinpoint the common drawbacks of the State pattern, because managing states are fundamental to game development, so we could say that this pattern is essential and cannot be disregarded.

The following are the benefits of using the State pattern:

- **Encapsulated behaviors**: The State pattern allows us to implement an entity's behaviors as a collection of self-contained components that can be attached dynamically to an object when it changes states.
- **Reduction of condition blocks**: Using the State pattern reduces the need for huge chunks of if-else conditions or switching cases, because behaviors can be dynamically assigned depending on an object's internal or global state change.

There is only one drawback:

- **Code complexity**: Implementing patterns sometimes results in verbose code bases with a higher number of classes because of encapsulation and highly defined structures

Use case example

Imagine we are working on a game in which the player controls a spaceship. Our lead designer is still brainstorming ideas on what exactly the spaceship will be able to do in our game. But they ask us to implement at least three core states that our spaceship could be in depending on the result of a space battle against an enemy ship:

- **Normal**: The player's spaceship is running as normal
- **Alert**: An enemy spaceship is approaching and is ready to attack
- **Disabled**: The player's spaceship has been defeated in battle and currently cannot move or fight back

In each state, there's a specific set of behaviors and actions for the crew members to perform:

- **Normal**: The crew members go into their default positions and perform their assigned duties
- **Alert**: The crew members run to their assigned combat positions
- **Disabled**: The crew members run to the escape pods and abandon the ship

The most important thing about this list is that it's very generic, which means that we could write those states and behaviors so, we can attach them to any type of ship in our game, including enemy ships. As we will see in the following code example, the State pattern permits us to decouple behaviors from entities, and this is why we can easily have an entity switch between states.

Code example

As described in the use case example, we are going to implement a finite series of states for our spaceship:

1. Let's start by implementing the interface that will be used to define our states:

```
public interface IShipState
{
    void Execute(Ship ship);
}
```

As you can see, the Execute function receives an entity of the Ship type. This declaration means that we will able to attach and execute our state on any ship, making our code very modular and extendable.

2. Now we are going to define each state and add some contextual code to the Execute() method:

```
public class NormalShipState : IShipState
{
    public void Execute(Ship ship)
    {
        ship.LogStatus("NORMAL: ship operating as normal.");
    }
}
```

The Normal state is our default one, which executes the behaviors of a normally operating ship.

3. Next is the `Alert` state. In this context, the crew of the ship and its system are alerted:

```
public class AlertShipState : IShipState
{
    public void Execute(Ship ship)
    {
        ship.LogStatus("ALERT: all hands on deck.");
    }
}
```

4. Finally, there is the `Disabled` state. This means that the ship is unable to move and the crew is fleeing:

```
public class DisabledShipState : IShipState
{
    public void Execute(Ship ship)
    {
        ship.LogStatus("DISABLED: crew jumping ship.");
    }
}
```

For our code example, we are making things straightforward by merely implementing some console outputs to indicate the current state, but in a real project, we could easily trigger sound cues, particles, and animations for every state change.

5. Now that we have a collection of states that we can attach to a ship. For the next step, let's write a concrete implementation of the `Ship` class:

```
using UnityEngine;

public class Ship : MonoBehaviour
{
    private IShipState m_CurrentState;

    void Awake ()
    {
        m_CurrentState = new NormalShipState();
        m_CurrentState.Execute(this);
    }

    public void Normalize()
    {
        m_CurrentState = new NormalShipState();
        m_CurrentState.Execute(this);
    }
```

```
    public void TriggerRedAlert()
    {
        m_CurrentState = new AlertShipState();
        m_CurrentState.Execute(this);
    }

    public void DisableShip()
    {
        m_CurrentState = new DisabledShipState();
        m_CurrentState.Execute(this);
    }

    public void LogStatus(string status)
    {
        Debug.Log(status);
    }
}
```

Let's review a short list of what we have accomplished with this pattern:

- We have eliminated the need for switch cases or if-elses to manage the transition between the ship's stateful behaviors.
- We have decoupled the ship's behaviors into self-contained components that we can attach dynamically to any type of ship.

These small benefits have given us a considerable amount of flexibility, and we can now write behaviors as individual components. This means we could have one colleague working on the Alert state while another refactors the Disabled state, without interfering with each other's work.

6. And the final part of our code example is our Client, a class that we will use to test each state by triggering them with the user's input:

```
using UnityEngine;

public class Client : MonoBehaviour
{
    public Ship ship;

    void Update()
    {
        if (Input.GetKeyDown("n"))
        {
            ship.Normalize();
        }
        if (Input.GetKeyDown("a"))
        {
```

```
        ship.TriggerRedAlert();
    }

    if (Input.GetKeyDown("d"))
    {
        ship.DisableShip();
    }
  }
}
```

In this example, we are manually triggering the ship's finite states, but we could have easily used events or a health system to trigger them. In other words, by using the State pattern, we have been given the flexibility to attach multiple stateful behaviors to any entity and trigger them dynamically through any type of mechanism, without having to write long and complex conditional statements.

Summary

In this chapter, we reviewed a pattern that's the cornerstone of game development. We now have the ability to encapsulate stateful behaviors into individual components that can be assigned dynamically to an object depending on its state. We have reduced our dependency on long conditional statements and have a consistent approach to structuring our code that's related to behaviors and state management.

In the next chapter, we are going to review the Visitor pattern, a unique pattern that gives us the ability to decouple algorithms from an object's structure.

Exercises

A conventional technique in video games to make entities feel less mechanical in the way they behave is to ease out the transition between states. For example: instead of having a patrolling enemy character transitioning immediately from a passive to an aggressive state when they detect the player's character, there could be a short animation sequence in between states, showing the enemy going into an alert stance before attacking.

As an exercise, I would recommend experimenting with the concept of integrating transitional states between each finite state of the spaceship and find a solution to make the transition between them blend seamlessly.

Further reading

Design Patterns: Elements of Reusable Object-Oriented Software, by Erich Gamma, John Vlissides, Ralph Johnson, and Richard Helm
(http://www.informit.com/store/design-patterns-elements-of-reusable-object-oriented-9780201633610)

11
Visitor

I have to admit that I find the Visitor pattern confusing and strange. I wrestled with the concepts behind this pattern for a while before grasping its design, mostly because I seldom use it, and I mostly read about it from academic sources. But I began to appreciate this pattern when I started to visualize objects not just as chunks of data stored in the heap, but as a structure that can be visited and acted upon by another object. So, this means that it's possible to perform specific operations on elements of an object's structure without modifying it. This approach can be useful when you need to implement a system that needs to traverse a hierarchical structure and execute specific operations on individual nodes.

The following topics will be covered in this chapter:

- The basic principles behind the Visitor pattern
- Implementing a simulation of a one-armed factory robot

Technical requirements

This chapter is hands-on. You will need to have a basic understanding of Unity and C#.

We will be using the following Unity engine and C# language concept:

- Interfaces

If you are unfamiliar with this concept, please review it before starting this chapter.

The code files of this chapter can be found on GitHub:

https://github.com/PacktPublishing/Hands-On-Game-Development-Patterns-with-Unity-2018

Check out the following video to see the code in action:

http://bit.ly/2OsR6d6

An overview of the Visitor pattern

The primary purpose of the Visitor pattern is simple once you grasp it; a *Visitable* object permits a Visitor object to operate on a specific element of its structure. This allows the visited object to receive new functionality from visitors.

This description might seem very abstract at first, but it's easier to visualize if you imagine an object as a data structure, instead of a closed-off container of data and logic. With this in mind, you can see that there's a broader array of possibilities in the way of manipulation objects.

In the following diagram, we can visualize those principals:

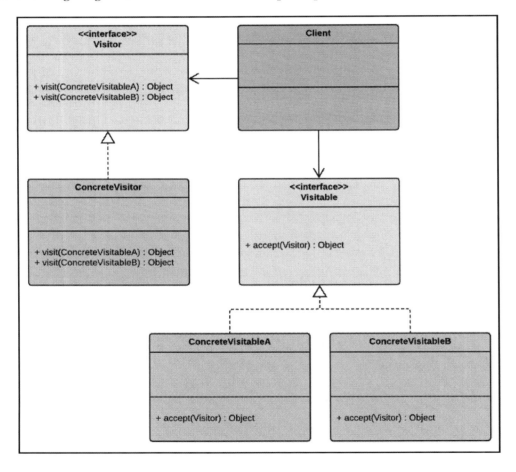

There are two key participants in this pattern:

- The **Visitor** is the interface for concrete visitors
- The **Visitable** is the interface for objects that are accepting visitors

Benefits and drawbacks

The Visitor pattern is not as popular as the singleton pattern or the dependency injection pattern, so there's less controversy surrounding its benefits and drawbacks, which are listed as follows:

The following are the benefits:

- **Separation of data and logic**: The Visitor pattern offers a way to decouple an object's data structures from its behaviors. This approach makes it easier to extend object capabilities by just adding more visitors.
- **Double dispatch**: The Visitor pattern offers the ability to choose which method to use at runtime, depending on a given argument's type, thereby making the code more dynamic.

The following are the drawbacks:

- **Code complexity**: The most obvious drawback of the Visitor pattern is that it makes code more obscure. A programmer that's not versed in the intricacies of the Visitor pattern might easily get lost.
- **Inflexibility**: The Visitor pattern is not an easy pattern to use, and demands consistency in its implementation. It can also be hard to remove once integrated into a code base, so it can be a long-term commitment.

Use case example

We will make our use case simple, so we don't get lost in layers of abstraction while we try to grasp the intricacies of the Visitor pattern. Imagine that we are working on a project in which we need to design an interactive simulation of a robot with a mechanical arm.

The robot is very modular, and primarily built out of various components. So, we want our code to reflect this by making it possible for us to attach individual components to our skeleton robot object dynamically. To achieve this, we are going to use the Visitor pattern, because it offers us a way to dynamically add elements to an object's structure without modifying it directly.

Code example

Now, it's time to implement our one-armed robot, by attaching to it all the components it needs to operate while not modifying its basic structure:

1. Let's start by implementing the Visitor interface, in which we declare those robot parts we are going to operate on with our Visitors:

```
public interface IRobotPartVisitor
{
    void Visit(Robot robot);
    void Visit(Battery battery);
    void Visit(MechanicalArm mechanicalArm);
    void Visit(ThermalImager thermalImager);
}
```

2. To help us out with our understanding of this pattern, let's implement two concrete Visitor patterns as follows; the first visits all our robot parts and turns them on, while the other one shuts them off:

   - RobotPartActivateVisitor:

```
using UnityEngine;

public class RobotPartActivateVisitor : IRobotPartVisitor
{
    public void Visit(Robot robot)
    {
        Debug.Log("Robot waking up.");
    }

    public void Visit(Battery battery)
    {
        Debug.Log("Battery is charged up.");
    }

    public void Visit(MechanicalArm mechanicalArm)
    {
        Debug.Log("The mechanical arm is actiaved.");
    }

    public void Visit(ThermalImager thermalImager)
    {
        Debug.Log("The thermal imager is turned on.");
    }
}
```

* `RobotPartShutdownVisitor:`

```csharp
using UnityEngine;

public class RobotPartShutdownVisitor : IRobotPartVisitor
{
    public void Visit(Robot robot)
    {
        Debug.Log("Robot is going back to sleep.");
    }

    public void Visit(Battery battery)
    {
        Debug.Log("Battery is charging down.");
    }

    public void Visit(MechanicalArm mechanicalArm)
    {
        Debug.Log("The mechanical arm is folding back to it's
default position.");
    }

    public void Visit(ThermalImager thermalImager)
    {
        Debug.Log("The thermal imager is turned off.");
    }
}
```

As you can see, it's quite straightforward at this point; we have a `Visit()` function for each robot part. This approach permits us to operate on them individually.

3. Now that we have our Visitors ready, it's time for us to implement our Visitables. Let's start by writing our `Visitable` interface:

```csharp
public interface IRobotPart
{
    void Accept(IRobotPartVisitor robotPartVisitor);
}
```

4. Let's now implement our concrete Visitables:

* `Battery:`

```csharp
public class Battery : IRobotPart
{
    public void Accept(IRobotPartVisitor robotPartVisitor)
```

```
    {
        robotPartVisitor.Visit(this);
    }
}
```

- ThermalImager:

```
public class ThermalImager : IRobotPart
{
    public void Accept(IRobotPartVisitor robotPartVisitor)
    {
        robotPartVisitor.Visit(this);
    }
}
```

- MechanicalArm:

```
public class MechanicalArm : IRobotPart
{
    public void Accept(IRobotPartVisitor robotPartVisitor)
    {
        robotPartVisitor.Visit(this);
    }
}
```

Notice how we are referencing the Visitor interface inside the `Accept()` function. This piece of code is what makes it possible for our Visitors to operate on our Visitables.

5. It's time for us to build our `Robot`, attaching all its core parts by referencing them in its constructor:

```
using UnityEngine;

public class Robot : IRobotPart
{
    private IRobotPart[] robotParts;

    public Robot()
    {
        robotParts = new IRobotPart[] { new MechanicalArm(), new
ThermalImager(), new Battery() };
    }

    public void Accept(IRobotPartVisitor robotPartVisitor)
    {
        for (int i = 0; i < robotParts.Length; i++)
        {
```

```
            robotParts[i].Accept(robotPartVisitor);
        }
        robotPartVisitor.Visit(this);
    }
}
```

6. Finally, we have our `Client` class, which acts as a proof of concept by actually triggering our Visitors to operate on our robot's parts:

```
using UnityEngine;

public class Client : MonoBehaviour
{
    void Update()
    {
        // Active robot
        if (Input.GetKeyDown(KeyCode.O))
        {
            IRobotPart robot = new Robot();
            robot.Accept(new RobotPartActivateVisitor());
        }
        // Shutdown robot
        if (Input.GetKeyDown(KeyCode.S))
        {
            IRobotPart robot = new Robot();
            robot.Accept(new RobotPartShutdownVisitor());
        }
    }
}
```

So, we have implemented a simple, but flexible, use case of the Visitor pattern. The point to bear in mind is that any Visitor can operate on a Visitable object if it has implemented the `Accept()` function. This mechanism allows various operations to be performed on a Visitable object without directly modifying it.

Summary

In this chapter, we reviewed the Visitor, probably one of the most advanced patterns in this book, because it demands that we approach object-oriented programming from a different perspective and start viewing objects as structures instead of abstract entities that exist on the heap. We can now use what we have learned and extend the Visitor pattern to implement systems that need to operate on complex hierarchical data structures, such as XML files or directory trees.

In the next chapter, we are going to review a handy, but straightforward, pattern that's often over-used in Unity, the Façade pattern.

Practical exercise

As a practical exercise, I would recommend studying an advanced use of the Visitor pattern. A perfect example of this is the application of the Visitor pattern to navigate and process an **Abstract Syntax Tree (AST)**. These types of implementations can showcase the architectural possibilities that the Visitor pattern offers.

For information on ASTs, please review the *Further reading* section.

Further reading

- *Dive Into Design Patterns,* by Alexander Shvets
  https://refactoring.guru/design-patterns/book
- *Abstract syntax tree*
  https://en.wikipedia.org/wiki/Abstract_syntax_tree

Section 5: Structural Patterns 5

In this section, we will explore Structural patterns, which will permit to us to adapt, extend, and connect game systems together that were built by various programmers so that we can reuse them in multiple projects. The design patterns in this book will teach you skills that will permit you to work with legacy code.

The following chapters are included in this section:

12
Facade

The Facade pattern is considered a Structural pattern so, as with most patterns of this type, it primarily focuses on identifying simple ways of establishing relationships between objects. The Facade pattern is an easy pattern to grasp because its name perfectly implies its design. The primary intent of the Facade pattern is to offer a simplified front-facing interface that abstracts the intricate inner workings of complex systems. This approach is beneficial for game developers because games are mostly constructed on layers of complexity and interacting systems.

The following topics will be covered in this chapter:

- We will be reviewing the basics of the Facade pattern
- We will use the Facade pattern to implement a save system

Technical requirements

This is a hands-on chapter, so you will need to have a basic understanding of Unity and C#.

We will be using the following specific Unity engine and C# language concepts:

- Singleton
- Serializable

If you're unfamiliar with these concepts, please review them before starting this chapter.

The code files of this chapter can be found on GitHub:

https://github.com/PacktPublishing/Hands-On-Game-Development-Patterns-with-Unity-2018

Check out the following video to see the code in action:

http://bit.ly/2I30suS

An overview of the Facade pattern

The Facade pattern's name is analogous to a facade in architecture—as the name implies, it's an exterior face that hides a complex structure. But, contrary to architecture, in software development, the goal of a Facade is not to beautify, but instead to simplify. As we are going to see in the following diagram, the implementation of the Facade pattern is usually limited to a single class that acts as a simplified interface to a complex array of interdependent sub-systems:

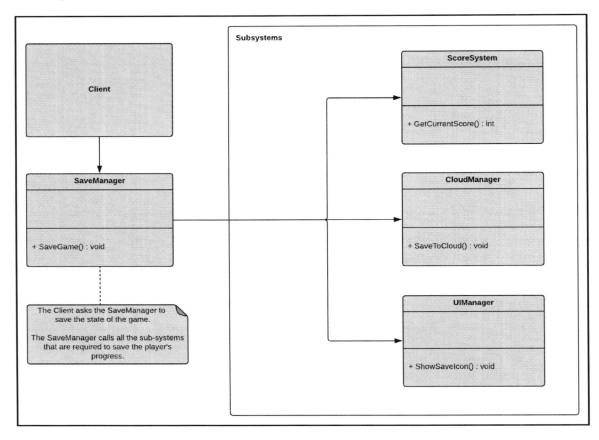

As we can see, when a client calls the `SaveGame()` function of `SaveManager`, there's a series of calls made to various dependencies and sub-systems (namely `ScoreSystem`, `CloudManager`, and `UIManager`). All of this happens behind the scenes; the client is unaware of the number of the sub-systems being called to complete his request. So, to save the current game's status, the client only needs to know that there's a single function in the `SaveManager` class, and the Facade pattern implementation does the rest behind the scenes.

Benefits and drawbacks

The Facade pattern has some substantial benefits, but can also present some long-term drawbacks:

The **benefits** are as follows:

- **Simplified interface to a complex body of code**: A solid Facade class will hide complexity and dependencies, while providing a simplified interface
- **Localization of all your dependency calls**: The Facade allows you to localize and group your dependencies into a single class
- **Easier refactoring**: Having complexity and dependency issues between sub-systems isolated in Facade classes simplifies the refactoring process, because you can refactor them in isolation without affecting clients, as the interfaces stay consistent

The following are some **drawbacks** to watch out for:

- **It makes it easier to hide the mess**: Having an excess of Facade classes can make it easier for programmers to disguise lousy code by making their architecture look simple to use, while brushing potential long-term architectural issues under the carpet.
- **Too many managers**: Manager classes are popular among Unity developers, and they often implement them by combining the Singleton and Facade patterns. This approach provokes an architecture that becomes an extensive collection of globally accessible managers. This type of design becomes very difficult to test and manage because the manager classes all become dependent on each other.

 The Facade establishes a new interface, whereas the Adapter recycles an old interface. It's important, when implementing patterns that might look and sound similar, to keep in mind that they're not necessarily identical in purpose.

An example use case

We are going to build a simple *save game* feature using a combination of the Facade and Singleton patterns. Our system has several steps that need to be executed in a specific sequence to complete the process of saving the player's progress. Here are the steps:

1. Trigger **User Interface (UI)** feedback to indicate the game is saving
2. Get the current player's data (health, score, ID)
3. Save the player's data to disk
4. Upload the save to the Cloud

We must respect the specific order of the preceding steps because we can't save to the disk before getting the current state of the player. But having to type each step manually in the right sequence every time we want to implement a save game event in our scripts can be time-consuming and error-prone. So, we are going to use the Facade pattern to establish a simple re-usable interface for our save game system.

A code example

As we are going to see, the Facade pattern is straightforward, so we will keep the following code example simple and straight to the point:

1. First off, we are going to write the classes for each of our sub-system examples:

   • `Player`: This class represents our player component:

   ```
   using UnityEngine;

   public class Player
   {
       public int GetHealth()
       {
           return 10;
       }

       public int GetPlayerID()
       {
           return 007;
       }
   }
   ```

- `ScoreManager`: This class is responsible for managing the scoring system; it will return the current player's score:

```
using UnityEngine;

public class ScoreManager
{
    public int GetScore(int playerId)
    {
        Debug.Log("Returning player score.");
        return 0;
    }
}
```

- `CloudManager`: This class is responsible for managing the cloud account of the current player, including uploading their local save data:

```
using UnityEngine;

public class CloudManager
{
    public void UploadSaveGame(string playerData)
    {
        Debug.Log("Uploading save data.");
    }
}
```

- `UIManager`: And finally, the UI manager is responsible for displaying the UI components:

```
using UnityEngine;

public class UIManager
{
    public void DisplaySaveIcon()
    {
        Debug.Log("Displaying the save icon.");
    }
}
```

2. Our next important class is a container that will hold the properties of the current player that we want to save. Notice that it's `Serializable`—this is because we are going to serialize an instance of this class when we save it to disk:

```
[System.Serializable]
class PlayerData
{
```

```
        public int score;
        public int playerID;
        public float health;
    }
```

3. Up next is the actual class that will act as our Facade. To avoid having a code example that's ten pages long, we are going to focus only on writing an elementary SaveManager class:

```
using System.IO;
using UnityEngine;
using System.Runtime.Serialization.Formatters.Binary;

public class SaveManager : Singleton<SaveManager>
{
    private UIManager m_UIManager;
    private PlayerData m_PlayerData;
    private ScoreManager m_ScoreManager;
    private CloudManager m_CloudManager;

    public void SaveGame(Player player)
    {
        // 1 - Show the save icon on the corner of the screen.
        m_UIManager = new UIManager();
        m_UIManager.DisplaySaveIcon();

        // 2 - Initializing a new Player Data.
        m_PlayerData = new PlayerData();
        m_PlayerData.health = player.GetHealth();
        m_PlayerData.playerID = player.GetPlayerID();

        // 3 - Getting the player's high score.
        m_ScoreManager = new ScoreManager();
        m_PlayerData.score =
m_ScoreManager.GetScore(player.GetPlayerID());
        // 4 - Let's serialize the player data.
        SerializePlayerData(m_PlayerData, true);
    }
    private void SerializePlayerData(PlayerData playerData, bool
isCloudSave)
    {
        // Serializing the PlayerData instance
        BinaryFormatter bf = new BinaryFormatter();
        FileStream file =
File.Create(Application.persistentDataPath + "/playerInfo.dat");
        bf.Serialize(file, playerData);
        file.Close();
        // Uploading the serialized playerInfo.dat file
```

```
        if (isCloudSave)
        {
                m_CloudManager = new CloudManager();
m_CloudManager.UploadSaveGame(Application.persistentDataPath +
"/playerInfo.dat");
        }
    }
}
```

As we can see, this small example of a `SaveManager` class presents a core problem: saving a player's progression has many steps and dependencies. Imagine if we had to write those steps by hand throughout our code every time we wanted to trigger a save game—this would be very difficult to maintain and debug.

4. We can see the benefits of the Facade pattern in action in the following `Client` class:

```
using UnityEngine;

public class Client : MonoBehaviour
{
    private Player m_Player;

    void Start()
    {
        m_Player = new Player();
    }

    void Update()
    {
        if (Input.GetKeyDown(KeyCode.S))
        {
            // Save the current player instance.
            SaveManager.Instance.SaveGame(m_Player);
        }
    }
}
```

Now, we can save the current player state from anywhere with just one line of code. This benefit is possible because our `SaveManager` is acting like a Facade and offering a simplified interface to a larger body of code. We have also localized the entire save game process so we can easily maintain it.

Summary

We now have the Facade pattern in our toolkit. It fits in perfectly with the reality of managing a complex code base that has an extensive collection of sub-systems that are constantly interacting with each other and are codependent, as in most video games. If the Facade pattern is used wisely, and not as a crutch or a way to mask messy code, it can become a cornerstone of your architecture. But the most critical point to keep in mind is that when you have a feature that relies on a collection of sub-systems to operate, it's a good idea to localize those dependencies so you can easily debug, maintain, and refactor them.

In the next chapter, we will explore the Adapter pattern, a close cousin of the Facade pattern, but with a very different design and intent.

Exercises

In this chapter, we wrote the first draft of a `SaveManager` class. As an exercise, try to write for yourself a complete save system for your game. It will be a valuable long-term investment if you design one that can be re-usable for multiple projects. From experience, I often witness game project's get into difficulty later on in their development cycle because they don't have a solid save and serialization system in place early on, so having one already prepared in your back pocket can very helpful.

Further reading

- *Game Programming Patterns* by Robert Nystrom, available here: http://gameprogrammingpatterns.com

13
Adapter

In a world full of different types of cables and plugs, we have all become accustomed to the concept of adapters. The Adapter pattern will be one of those patterns that will be easy for you to grasp, because it correlates so perfectly with our real-world experiences with technology. The Adapter pattern's name perfectly reveals its core purpose; it offers us a way to seamlessly use old code with new code by adding an interface between the code that will act as an Adapter.

The following topics will be covered in this chapter:

- We will review the basics of the Adapter pattern.
- We will use the Adapter pattern to adjust an online user management system without modifying any code.

Technical requirements

This chapter is a hands-on chapter; you will need to have a basic understanding of Unity and C#.

We will be using the following specific Unity engine and C# language concept:

- Sealed class

If you are unfamiliar with this concept, please review it before starting this chapter.

The code files of this chapter can be found on GitHub:

https://github.com/PacktPublishing/Hands-On-Game-Development-Patterns-with-Unity-2018

Check out the following video to see the code in action:

http://bit.ly/2UieM9v

An overview of the Adapter pattern

As its name implies, the Adapter pattern adapts two incompatible interfaces; like a plug adapter, it doesn't modify what it adjusts, but bridges one interface with another. This approach can be beneficial when you are dealing with legacy code that you cannot refactor due to its fragility.

They are two main approaches to implementing the Adapter pattern; here's a quick breakdown:

- **Object adapter**: A simple approach that uses composition
- **Class adapter**: A more advanced approach that uses inheritance

Trying to learn both at the same time can get confusing, so in this chapter, we will try to focus on the core purpose of the Adapter pattern by implementing an object adapter and briefly reviewing the class adapter afterward.

Let's take a look at a side-by-side diagram of the Object and Class adapters; the core differences can be subtle, but the similarities are apparent:

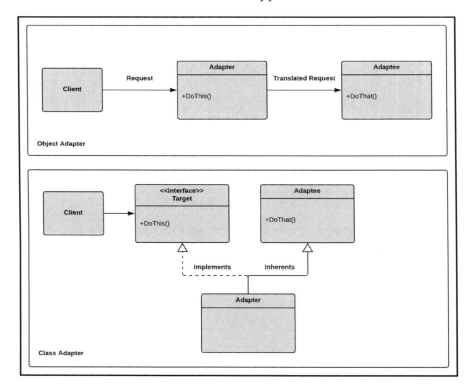

As you can see, in both cases, the **Adapter** class is positioned between the **Client** and the class that's being adapted (**Adaptee**). They only differ through their relationship to the **Adaptee**.

So, the core differences between the **Object** and **Class** adapters are as follows:

- The **Object Adapter** usually contains an instance of the **Adaptee** and translates the calls from the **Client** to the **Adaptee**; in other words, it acts slightly like a wrapper.
- The **Class Adapter** implements the expected interface while inheriting the **Adaptee**; it's a more advanced approach to adaption.

From experience, I have found that the Adapter pattern can sometimes be confused with the Facade pattern. It's essential we understand that the core difference between them is that the Facade pattern offers a simple interface to a complicated collection of interdependent sub-systems, while the Adapter pattern adapts an interface of another class so that it's consistent with the expectations of a client.

So, if you're attempting to adapt access to multiple classes with a singular interface, then you are probably implementing a Facade and not an Adapter.

Benefits and drawbacks

I don't consider the Adapter pattern a long-term solution to architecture issues; even though it offers some benefits, its long-term drawbacks should always be taken into consideration.

The following are the benefits:

- **Adapting without modifying**: The main benefit of the Adapter pattern is that it offers a standard approach to adapting code without modifying it.
- **Reusability and flexibility**: This pattern permits continuing to use legacy code with new systems with a minimal amount of changes; this has an immediate return on investment.

The following are the drawbacks:

- **Persisting legacy**: The ability to use legacy code with new systems is cost-effective, but in the long term, it can become an issue, because the old code might limit your upgrading options as it becomes deprecated and incompatible with new versions of Unity or third-party libraries.
- **Slight overhead**: Because you are redirecting calls between objects, there might be a slight performance hit.

 From experience, migrating code bases from one version of Unity to another can be quite time-consuming. So, don't be surprised if you end up having multiple versions of Unity installed on your computer so that you can maintain legacy code that's too expensive to upgrade.

Use case example

Let's suppose that we are dealing with a typical real-world game development scenario. Our lead online programmer is on vacation and has left explicit instructions that we should not make any modifications to his online player management system during his absence. However, our producer needs a change to our online components because he wants to showcase our live streaming service to a new investor.

To accomplish this in time, we will need to make changes; so, we have two choices:

- Modify the online player management system directly, even if we are not the owner of this section of the code base and don't understand it well.
- Find a way to extend the current system and implement the requested changes using a temporary adapter, which will limit the direct modification of our colleague's code.

With the Adapter pattern, we can implement the second option in a structured and consistent manner. In the next section, we will apply this use case with a straightforward example, which will undoubtedly showcase the usefulness of this pattern.

Code example

As we have mentioned, we are going to implement a change to our online player management system by adapting the `OnlinePlayer` class, without modifying it directly. The example is straightforward, but from experience, it's always better to learn a new pattern by implementing the simplest systems first.

For reasons of brevity, we are going to adapt the way the following `OnlinePlayer` class returns the full name of a specific player. Let's keep in mind that we can't refactor or extend this class; we can only adapt it. We will do this by using these two primary forms of the Adapter pattern:

- Object adapter
- Class adapter

Object adapter

The following `OnlinePlayer` class can return the first and last name of an online player, as well as their full name. However, the programmer that implemented the class decided to return the string in a formal naming structure. We need to have the full name in a standard sequence, which is the first then the last name.

Of course, we could call the first and last name GET functions individually, and then concatenate them together in our client, but this means that we will have to do it everywhere that we might need to get a user's full name. In other words, we lose consistency and localized control of how the full name is returned. You can imagine how this could become risky if we were to adapt something more complex, such as an in-game currency transaction system:

```
public sealed class OnlinePlayer : ScriptableObject
{
    public string GetFirstName(int id)
    {
        // Lookup online database.
        return "John"; // Retun a placeholder name.
    }

    public string GetLastName(int id)
    {
        // Lookup online database.
        return "Doe"; // Return a placeholder last name.
    }

    public string GetFullName(int id)
    {
        // Lookup online database and get full name
        return "Doe Jonn";
    }
}
```

There's something else important to note in the `OnlinePlayer` class; it's `sealed`, which means that we can't use it as a base class. As a consequence, we can't extend it directly, so adapting it is our only option:

1. Let's build an adapter class that will fix our issue with the `GetFullName()` function:

```
using UnityEngine;

public class OnlinePlayerObjectAdapter : ScriptableObject
{
    public string GetFullName(OnlinePlayer onlinePlayer, int userId)
    {
        return onlinePlayer.GetFirstName(userId) + " " + onlinePlayer.GetLastName(userId);
    }
}
```

As you can see, the `OnlinePlayerObjectAdapter` class receives an instance of the `OnlinePlayer` class and wraps the `GetFullName()` method, so it returns the expected full name format. So, we are not modifying or extending the behavior of the class that's being adapted, but are merely adjusting it to the client's expectations.

2. Let's implement a `Client` class in order to test our implementation:

```
using UnityEngine;

public class Client : MonoBehaviour
{
    private OnlinePlayer m_OnlinePlayer;
    private OnlinePlayerObjectAdapter m_OnlinePlayerAdapter;

    void Update()
    {
        if (Input.GetKeyDown(KeyCode.U))
        {
            m_OnlinePlayer =
ScriptableObject.CreateInstance<OnlinePlayer>();
            m_OnlinePlayerAdapter =
ScriptableObject.CreateInstance<OnlinePlayerObjectAdapter>();

            string FirstName = m_OnlinePlayer.GetFirstName(79);
            string LastName = m_OnlinePlayer.GetLastName(79);

            string FullNameLastFirst =
```

```
m_OnlinePlayer.GetFullName(79);
            string FullNameFirstLast =
m_OnlinePlayerAdapter.GetFullName(m_OnlinePlayer, 79);

            Debug.Log(FirstName);
            Debug.Log(LastName);
            Debug.Log(FullNameLastFirst);
            Debug.Log(FullNameFirstLast);
        }
    }
}
```

Now that we have an adapter, we have access to the OnlinePlayer class's original implementation of the GetFullName() function, and also an adapted version of it. This approach offers us a lot of flexibility with minimal risk, because we are not modifying anything, but are merely adapting.

In this section, we implemented a simple example of the object adapter. In the next section, we will review a sophisticated approach to the adapter by implementing a class adapter.

Class adapter

There's one detail that we are going to modify in our OnlinePlayer class for this section; we are going to remove the sealed modifier, because we want to be able to inherit the OnlinePlayer class. So, let's pretend that it was never there in the first place:

```
public class OnlinePlayer : ScriptableObject
{
    public string GetFirstName(int id)
    {
        // Lookup online database.
        return "John"; // Retun a placeholder name.
    }

    public string GetLastName(int id)
    {
        // Lookup online database.
        return "Doe"; // Return a placeholder last name.
    }

    public string GetFullName(int id)
    {
        // Lookup online database and pull the full name in this sequence
[Last Name & First Name].
        return "Doe Jonn";
```

```
        }
    }
```

To implement the class adapter approach, let's follow a step-by-step procedure:

1. Let's start by implementing a target interface for our clients; we are going to call it IOnlinePlayer:

    ```
    public interface iOnlinePlayer
    {
        string GetFirstName(int userID);
        string GetLastName(int userID);
        string GetFullNameLastFirst(int userID);
        string GetFullNameFirstLast(int userID);
    }
    ```

    You should notice that we are adapting the OnlinePlayer class by adding a new interface that will expose the new functionality for the class that we are improving. This approach is flexible, as you will see in the following steps.

2. Now, in our adapter class, we are going to implement the IOnliePlayer interface:

    ```
    public class OnlinePlayerClassAdapter : OnlinePlayer, iOnlinePlayer
    {
        public string GetFullNameLastFirst(int userId)
        {
            return GetFullName(userId);
        }

        public string GetFullNameFirstLast(int userId)
        {
            return GetFirstName(userId) + " " + GetLastName(userId);
        }
    }
    ```

    It looks simple, but there are a lot of things going on. Let's try to unwrap this:

    *   OnlinePlayerClassAdapter is implementing the IOnlinePlayer interface.
    *   OnlinePlayerClassAdapter is also inheriting the OnlinePlayer class.
    *   Because we are inheriting the OnlinePlayer class, GetFirstName() and GetLastName() are implemented by default.
    *   OnlinePlayerClassAdapter only needs to explicitly implement GetFullNameLastFirst() and GetFullNameFirstLast().

- `GetFullNameLastFirst()` redirects the call to `GetFullName()`, implemented inside the `OnlinePlayer` parent class.
- `GetFullNameFirstLast()` actually adapts the way that we return a full name to a client.

3. Let's look at how we can use this to our advantage with a `Client` class:

```
using UnityEngine;

public class Client : MonoBehaviour
{
    private iOnlinePlayer m_OnlinePlayer;

    void Update()
    {
        if (Input.GetKeyDown(KeyCode.U))
        {
            m_OnlinePlayer =
ScriptableObject.CreateInstance<OnlinePlayerClassAdapter>();

            string FirstName = m_OnlinePlayer.GetFirstName(79);
            string LastName = m_OnlinePlayer.GetLastName(79);

            string FullNameLastFirst =
m_OnlinePlayer.GetFullNameLastFirst(79);
            string FullNameFirstLast=
m_OnlinePlayer.GetFullNameFirstLast(79);

            Debug.Log(FirstName);
            Debug.Log(LastName);
            Debug.Log(FullNameLastFirst);
            Debug.Log(FullNameFirstLast);
        }
    }
}
```

We have decoupled the client from the adapted class because we only need to point it towards the adapter during the assignment of the `m_OnlinePlayer` member variable. For the client, the interaction with the adapted `OnlinePlayer` class is relatively transparent and is consistent with the previous implementations.

In other words, we were able to adapt the `OnlinePlayer` class without modifying it while maintaining a consistent interface. That's the core purpose of the Adapter pattern.

Summary

In this chapter, we added the Adapter pattern to our toolbox. It's a type of pattern that's very useful in the field, because one of the biggest challenges for a professional programmer is dealing with legacy code, which is often maintained by people you don't know. So, having a consistent approach to adapting other peoples' code without causing regression with unnecessary changes is the secret to a long career and a good reputation.

In the next chapter, we will review the decorator, a more complex and advanced structural pattern.

Exercises

In this chapter, we implemented a straightforward use case of the Adapter pattern, but its return on investment is in adapting legacy code into a new context. As an exercise, I recommend looking into your Unity projects and finding components or systems that you could adapt from one project to another without modifying them.

Further reading

- *Game Programming Patterns* by Robert Nystrom: `http://gameprogrammingpatterns.com`

14
Decorator

The Decorator is one of those rare patterns where the name represents its purpose perfectly. As its name implies, the Decorator pattern permits us to decorate an object; this is, of course, a very vague explanation. So, a more concrete but simple explanation of its core purpose is that it offers us a way to decorate old code with new code, by dynamically adding functionality to an object.

The following topics will be covered in this chapter:

- We will review the basics of the Decorator pattern
- We will build a system to add attachments to a rifle dynamically

Technical requirements

This chapter is hands-on, so you will need to have a basic understanding of Unity and C#.

We will be using the following specific Unity engine and C# language concept:

- Constructors

If you are unfamiliar with this concept, please review it before starting this chapter.

The code files of this chapter can be found on GitHub:

https://github.com/PacktPublishing/Hands-On-Game-Development-Patterns-with-Unity-2018

Check out the following video to see the code in action:

http://bit.ly/2U0MT6x

The basics of the Decorator pattern

The Decorator pattern is the type of pattern that you would need to implement in code in order to fully understand, so we are going to keep the theory section brief. In its most basic form, the Decorator pattern offers us a mechanism that permits us to add behaviors to objects at runtime without altering the objects in the process.

As its name implies, it decorates objects; but it does so by chaining references of decorator objects through the constructor of a base class. It might sound abstract, but in practice it works, because of the way objects refer to each other in memory.

Let's look at the following diagram in order to visualize the relationship structure between classes in the Decorator pattern:

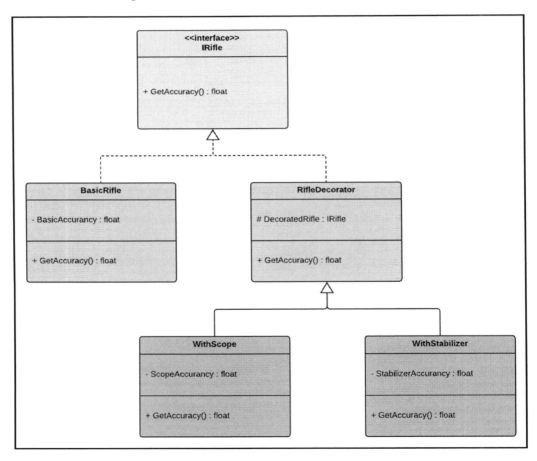

As you can see, there's an interface, `IRifle`, which is offering an implementation contract to all classes that want to be rifles. But, the most important class in the diagram is the `RifleDecorator`. It's the class that will permit us to attach the `WithScope` and `WithStabilizer` decorators to any rifle object that implements `IRifle`.

But, before writing this in code, let's review some of the core benefits and possible drawbacks when using the Decorator pattern.

Benefits and drawbacks

The Decorator pattern has an excellent reputation; it's even a significant part of the Python language. So, its benefits often outweigh its drawbacks, as we can see in the following list:

The following are the benefits:

- **Alternative to subclassing**: The Decorator pattern focuses on injecting functionality into an object, instead of inheriting and then extending.
- **Manageable permutations**: Features and requirements change all the time during production; the Decorator pattern offers a way to add functionality by distributing it through self-contained components, without modifying core implementations.
- **Runtime dynamics**: The Decorator pattern permits us to add functionality to an object at runtime without modifying it directly.

The following are the drawbacks:

- **Code complexity**: Like most advanced patterns, implementing the Decorator pattern can result in a more complex code base.
- **Relationship complexity**: Keeping track of the chain of initialization and the relationships between decorators can become very complicated if there are multiple layers of decorators around an object.

 The drawbacks of specific patterns are often related to the complexity and verbosity they add to a code base. It's mostly an issue when working in a team of members with various levels of experience, because junior programmers might not have the skills to recognize specific patterns just by reading the code.

Use case example

Weapons are an essential element of video games, especially in the first-person shooter (FPS) genre. A very cool and profitable feature to have in an FPS is weapon customization. The ability to upgrade a basic rifle by attaching new components to it, such as a scope or silencer, is very engaging. But, as a game programmer, having to write all these variations and configurations in code, in a structured and modular manner, can be very complicated.

But, with the Decorator pattern, we can reproduce the real-life concept of attaching components to a configurable weapon in code. This is what we are going to do in the following code example.

 The Adapter and Decorator patterns are similar, but Adapter is used to adapt an object's interface, while Decorator enhances an object's responsibilities.

Code example

A particular thing to keep in mind in the following code example is that we are going to use constructors. It's often recommended not to use them in Unity, because if you are working with `Monobehaviours` or `ScritableObjects` derived classes and you attach them to `GameObjects` included in a scene, the engine will automatically initialize them. But, in this example, we are going to break this rule; mainly because the Decorator is dependent on the internal mechanisms of the constructor, as we are going to see in the following code snippets:

1. Let's begin the implementation of our weapon customization system by writing an interface that will be used as an *implementation contract* for all our derived rifle types:

```
public interface IRifle
{
    float GetAccuracy();
}
```

As we can see, it's a simple interface with one function that returns the accuracy value of a rifle as a float.

2. Now that we have a standard interface for all our rifle objects, let's write a concrete rifle class that will represent a basic configuration of a rifle:

```
public class BasicRifle : IRifle
{
    private float m_BasicAccurancy = 5.0f;

    public float GetAccuracy()
    {
        return m_BasicAccurancy;
    }
}
```

The BasicRifle class is doing nothing special; it just implements the IRifle interface; but we are going to use it as a foundation object that we are going to decorate with attachments that will upgrade its default accuracy.

3. We now need a class that will take the responsibility of attaching the decorators to our BasicRifle object:

```
abstract public class RifleDecorator : IRifle
{
    protected IRifle m_DecoaratedRifle;

    public RifleDecorator(IRifle rifle)
    {
        m_DecoaratedRifle = rifle;
    }

    public virtual float GetAccuracy()
    {
        return m_DecoaratedRifle.GetAccuracy();
    }
}
```

We are implementing the core of the Decorator pattern in the RifleDecorator class. We can see that the RifleDecorator class is implementing the IRifle interface, but there's a small detail that's very important to notice. The GetAccuracy() function is virtual, which means that any derived class of RifleDecorator will be able to override it.

4. Now that we have our Decorator class, let's see how an actual decorator object will attach itself to our `BasicRifle` object during runtime:

```
public class WithScope : RifleDecorator
{
    private float m_ScopeAccurancy = 20.0f;
    // Constructor
    public WithScope(IRifle rifle) : base(rifle) {}

    public override float GetAccuracy()
    {
        return base.GetAccuracy() + m_ScopeAccurancy;
    }
}
```

The first thing to notice is the constructor; it takes an `IRifle` type object as an argument, and then calls its base constructor. This approach might seem very tangled at first view, but it's going to become clear once we implement the client side of this example. Another detail to note is that we are overriding the `GetAccuracy()` function, but also changing the overall accuracy of the rifle by adding `m_ScopeAccurancy` to the base value in the return path.

5. To showcase the flexibility of the Decorator pattern, let's add another decorator to our example:

```
public class WithStabilizer : RifleDecorator
{
    private float m_StabilizerAccurancy = 10.0f;
    // Constructor
    public WithStabilizer(IRifle rifle) : base(rifle) {}

    public override float GetAccuracy()
    {
        return base.GetAccuracy() + m_StabilizerAccurancy;
    }
}
```

`WithStabilizer` has the same implementation as the `WithScope`, except for the final accuracy value that it returns.

6. Now, it's time to implement the client; this is where we are going to trigger the decoration feature of the Decorator pattern:

```
using UnityEngine;

public class Client : MonoBehaviour
{
    void Update()
    {
        if (Input.GetKeyDown("b"))
        {
            IRifle rifle = new BasicRifle();
            Debug.Log("Basic accuracy: " + rifle.GetAccuracy());
        }

        if (Input.GetKeyDown("s"))
        {
            IRifle rifle = new BasicRifle();
            rifle = new WithScope(rifle);
            Debug.Log("WithScope accuracy: " +
rifle.GetAccuracy());
        }

        if (Input.GetKeyDown("t"))
        {
            IRifle rifle = new BasicRifle();
            rifle = new WithScope(new WithStabilizer(rifle));
            Debug.Log("Stabilizer+Scope accuracy: " +
            rifle.GetAccuracy());
        }
    }
}
```

The most important element to notice in this class is the chaining of the constructor calls in the following line:

```
rifle = new WithScope(new WithStabilizer(rifle));
```

With this line of code, we are basically attaching the `WithScope` and `WithStabilizer` decorators to a `BasicRifle` instance by chaining them with the base constructor.

So, we can now get different accuracy outputs depending on how many attachments we attach to the `BasicRifle` instance, as follows.

The following code returns accuracy of `5.0f`:

```
IRifle rifle = new BasicRifle();
rifle.GetAccuracy();
```

The following code returns accuracy of `25.0f`:

```
IRifle rifle = new WithScope(rifle);
rifle.GetAccuracy();
```

The following code returns accuracy of `35.0f`:

```
IRifle rifle = new WithScope(new WithStabilizer(rifle));
rifle.GetAccuracy();
```

So, by using the Decorator pattern, we now have an underlying implementation of a dynamic weapon customization system that we can extend to build a collection of runtime attachments for our game's weaponry.

Summary

In this chapter, we reviewed a pattern that offers a game programmer a flexible way to implement an often requested feature – weapon customization. It appears that the Decorator pattern was perfectly designed to accomplish this type of task. But, as you can imagine, the Decorator can be used to implement all kinds of customizable systems and features, such as the following:

- Vehicle upgrades
- Armour and clothing

In the next chapter, we will transition out of Behavioral patterns and will instead focus on Decouplers, starting with the Event Bus.

Practice

In this chapter, we decided to use native C# constructors, which is proper because we were not using `MonoBehaviours` or `ScritableObjects`. But this not always the case, so, as an exercise, you should try to refactor the code example we just completed, but without any constructors and primarily using native Unity `MonoBehaviours` and `ScriptableObjects`.

You can find hints on how to accomplish this in the official Unity API documentation on `ScriptableObjects`; please check the *Further reading* section for more information.

Further reading

- *Unity – Scripting API: ScriptableObject*
  https://docs.unity3d.com/ScriptReference/ScriptableObject.html
- *Design Patterns: Elements of Reusable Object-Oriented Software* by Erich Gamma, John Vlissides, Ralph Johnson, and Richard Helm
  http://www.informit.com/store/design-patterns-elements-of-reusable-object-oriented-9780201633610

Section 6: Decoupling Patterns 6

Unity might have a robust built-in component system, but it won't prevent you from having tight coupling issues in your code base. You want to make sure objects can communicate with each other without being bound together to the point that if one element is missing in the chain, everything breaks down. The patterns in this section are designed to help you decouple your dependencies and offer a way to write code that's more scalable.

The following chapters are included in this section:

15
Event Bus

For our first subject in the *Decoupling* section of this book, we are going to review the Event Bus pattern. But first, we need to address the confusion that often arises between the definition of an Event Bus and its close cousin, the Event Queue. We can quickly boil down the core difference between both from their names.

A bus permits data to flow between different components, while a queue collects a list of data that needs processing at sequential intervals. And by this high-level definition of a bus, we can conclude that an Event Bus will focus on serving as a central hub for the publishing and broadcasting of events, and not as a queue of those events.

So, in this chapter, we will be focusing on building an Event Bus that will optimize the way we decouple listeners and consumers of events in Unity.

The following topics will be covered in this chapter:

- Reviewing the basics of the Event Bus pattern
- Implementing a global messaging system that can be adapted to any game

Technical requirements

The Event Bus is an extension of the Observer pattern, so I recommend revisiting `Chapter 10`, *Observer*, before starting this one.

We will also be using the following specific Unity engine API features:

- `UnityEvents`
- `UnityActions`

If you're unfamiliar with these, please review their official Unity API documentation, but note that we will be reviewing them in the *Code example* section of this chapter.

The code files of this chapter can be found on GitHub:

```
https://github.com/PacktPublishing/Hands-On-Game-Development-Patterns-with-
Unity-2018
```

Check out the following video to see the code in action:

```
http://bit.ly/2OxHxto
```

An overview of the Event Bus Pattern

There's a possible point of confusion around the Event Bus pattern. It's sometimes referred to as a **Messaging System** or the **Publish-Subscribe** pattern, the latter being the most accurate name for what we are implementing in this chapter. But because we are taking a very hands-on approach to this book, we are going to refer to this pattern's design as an Event Bus, which is a more high-level and system-oriented name for it.

As we have seen in `Chapter 9`, *Observer*, C# has native implementations that simplify the process of integrating events by offering an event-driven mechanism that permits Subjects and Observers to communicate with each other. But C#'s native event system does have a drawback – observers need to be *aware* of the presence of potential subjects, or unexpected behaviors can occur.

This, therefore, is why we are going to learn how to use the Event Bus—with this pattern, we are going to eliminate this dependency and make it possible for any object to publish events and subscribe to them without any direct dependencies between each other. Consequently, we will shift from an observer/subject arrangement to a more flexible publisher/subscriber approach.

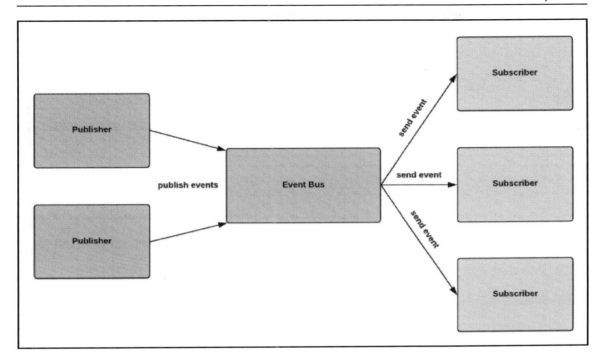

Let's review the following diagram of the Event Bus and examine its elements:

As we can see, there are three main ingredients:

- **Publishers**: These objects can request the hub to manage specific events and broadcast them to the right listeners
- **Event Hub**: This object is responsible for coordinating the communication of events between the **Publishers** and **Subscribers**
- **Subscribers**: These objects subscribe themselves to the hub's event broadcast channel so they can listen for specific events

Benefits and drawbacks

The benefits and drawbacks of the Event Bus are quite moderate—it's a pattern that permits the implementation of an event management system without asking for significant architectural changes in your code base:

The **benefits** are as follows:

- **Decouples systems**: Because publishers and subscribers only communicate through the Event Bus, it reduces direct references and decouples objects from each other
- **Broadcast channels**: Similar to a TV or radio broadcast system, you can use the Event Bus as a way to transmit messages through specific channels that listeners can subscribe to at their discretion

The **drawbacks** to be aware of are as follows:

- **Memory overhead**: Under the hood of any event system, there's a lot of low-level memory mechanisms that are being triggered to manage the communication between objects, so it might not be the best choice if you need to squeeze milliseconds of processing out of every frame

An example use case

Unlike other patterns in this book, the Event Bus is a functional and complete system in itself. This fact means that we can implement it without having to map it into a specific in-game system, and it will still become an instrumental component of our game's architecture.

We could almost view the Event Bus as a global service that offers a way for all our components to message each other on specific channels. So, in the *Code example* section, we are going to implement the Event Bus in its native form, and make sure that it's globally accessible as a service for all our components.

 Before starting the *Code example* section, I recommend reviewing Chapter 6, *Singleton*, because we are going to use it as a base for our Event Bus class.

Code example

As mentioned in the *An example use case* section, we are going to implement the Event Bus as a service that all our components will be able to use when they need to broadcast events to other objects.

So, let's start by implementing the core of the system by writing our Event Bus class:

```
using UnityEngine.Events;
using System.Collections.Generic;

public class EventBus : Singleton<EventBus>
{
    private Dictionary<string, UnityEvent> m_EventDictionary;

    public override void Awake()
    {
        base.Awake();
        Instance.Init();
    }

    private void Init()
    {
        if (Instance.m_EventDictionary == null)
        {
            Instance.m_EventDictionary = new Dictionary<string,
UnityEvent>();
        }
    }

    public static void StartListening(string eventName, UnityAction
listener)
    {
        UnityEvent thisEvent = null;
        if (Instance.m_EventDictionary.TryGetValue(eventName, out
thisEvent))
        {
            thisEvent.AddListener(listener);
        }
        else
        {
            thisEvent = new UnityEvent();
            thisEvent.AddListener(listener);
            Instance.m_EventDictionary.Add(eventName, thisEvent);
        }
    }

    public static void StopListening(string eventName, UnityAction
listener)
    {
        UnityEvent thisEvent = null;
        if (Instance.m_EventDictionary.TryGetValue(eventName, out
thisEvent))
        {
```

```
                    thisEvent.RemoveListener(listener);
            }
        }

        public static void TriggerEvent(string eventName)
        {
            UnityEvent thisEvent = null;
            if (Instance.m_EventDictionary.TryGetValue(eventName, out
thisEvent))
            {
                thisEvent.Invoke();
            }
        }
    }
```

As we can see, we are making our class into a Singleton; this will permit our EventBus instance to be globally accessible. But the most critical element that we need to notice is that we are using two new specific Unity API features: UnityEvent and UnityAction.

UnityEvent and UnityAction are API wrappers over the .NET native delegate type. They behave almost exactly like regular delegates under the hood, but they offer extra features that are custom to Unity, such as the following, for example:

- Inspector access
- Persistent callbacks

We are using them in our example for reasons of simplicity while making sure we exploit Unity API's features to the fullest.

 For more detailed information on the specific features that UnityEvent offers, please refer the official API documentation in the *Further reading* section.

If we break down the class even further, we can see that four core functions make the Event Hub function:

- Init(): This initializes a dictionary that will hold in memory events to which Subscribers register
- StartListening(): This is a function that Listeners uses to register themselves to listen to a specific event

- `StopListening()`: This function permits `Listeners` to stop listening to a specific event
- `TriggerEvent()`: This function will trigger an event and broadcast it to all its `Listeners`

In theory, our work is done—with one class, we were able to implement an Event Bus that's globally accessible and ready to manage the communication of events between objects. So now, the only thing to do is to write ourselves an example of a Publisher object, along with a couple of Subscribers to test our new Event Bus service.

Let's start with the Publisher, as without one, our `Listeners` will have nothing to listen to except silence. We are going to implement a straightforward Publisher that triggers a broadcast of specific events depending on user input:

```
using UnityEngine;

public class EventPublisher : MonoBehaviour
{
    void Update()
    {
        if (Input.GetKeyDown("s"))
        {
            EventBus.TriggerEvent("Shoot");
        }

        if (Input.GetKeyDown("l"))
        {
            EventBus.TriggerEvent("Launch");
        }
    }
}
```

Our `EventPublisher` class is elementary—it asks the Event Hub to broadcast the `Launch` and `Shoot` events depending on user input. This implementation means that any `Listeners` that are listening for events named `Launch` or `Shoot` will be triggered.

To validate this functionality, let's implement two Listeners, each with different responsibilities:

- `Rocket`: This class listens for a `Launch` command event, and when it receives it, it triggers a launch sequence:

    ```
    using UnityEngine;

    public class Rocket : MonoBehaviour
    ```

```
{
    private bool m_IsQuitting;
    private bool m_IsLaunched = false;

    void OnEnable()
    {
        EventBus.StartListening("Launch", Launch);
    }

    void OnApplicationQuit()
    {
        m_IsQuitting = true;
    }

    void OnDisable()
    {
        if (m_IsQuitting == false)
        {
            EventBus.StopListening("Launch", Launch);
        }
    }

    void Launch()
    {
        if (m_IsLaunched == false)
        {
            m_IsLaunched = true;
            Debug.Log("Received a launch event : rocket
launching!");
        }
    }
}
```

- Cannon: Similar to the Rocket class, Cannon listens for a Shoot command and then triggers the shooting mechanism at the reception of the message:

```
using UnityEngine;

public class Cannon : MonoBehaviour
{
    private bool m_IsQuitting;

    void OnEnable()
    {
        EventBus.StartListening("Shoot", Shoot);
    }

    void OnApplicationQuit()
```

```
    {
        m_IsQuitting = true;
    }

    void OnDisable()
    {
        if (m_IsQuitting == false)
        {
            EventBus.StopListening("Shoot", Shoot);
        }
    }

    void Shoot()
    {
        Debug.Log("Received a shoot event : shooting cannon!");
    }
}
```

Listeners only need to register themselves as listeners of a specific event by calling the StartListening() function and specifying the name of the event they want to listen to, along with the callback function. The Event Bus will take responsibility for coordinating the broadcast of events to the right Listeners and trigger their respective callback function when required.

There's something else we need to address. Notice that we are checking if the application is quitting with OnApplicationQuit() and validating the Boolean value of m_IsQuitting for false before calling the EventBus.StopListening() function. This approach is to avoid calling objects that might not be in memory anymore once the application is quitting.

In conclusion, the Event Bus almost performs a similar function to a motherboard bus in the sense that it's acting like a system of communication between separate components. But even a simple Event Bus, like the one we just implemented, can be extended into a more complex system, such as an Event Queue or a multi-channel Messaging System, if need be.

Summary

In this chapter, we reviewed and implemented the Event Bus, a pattern with a focus on decoupling the relationship between the objects that broadcast events and those that listen to them. By exploiting new native Unity API features such as UnityEvents, we were able to implement this pattern with the minimum amount of code quickly.

In the next chapter, we will be reviewing the Service Locator, another pattern that focuses on decoupling complex relationships between dependencies, but this time by offering a way for objects to locate services.

 I encourage any Unity programmer to take the time to read the engine's entire API documentation, currently available on Unity's official website, and to memorize as much of it as you can. This exercise will make you more aware of the features it offers, and may even make you a faster coder. The detailed knowledge of this API will also impress your colleagues or potential future interviewers.

Exercise

As indicated at the beginning of this chapter, we decided to focus on the Event Bus pattern, and not its cousin, the Event Queue. But a bus mechanism can be converted to a queue. So, as a practical exercise, I would recommend to converting the Event Bus example we just completed, and instead of just having it forwarding triggered events to subscribers, it should hold them in a queue so they can be handled sequentially.

You can refer to the material indicated in the *Further reading* section of this chapter for inspiration.

Further reading

- *Unity - Manual: UnityEvents:*
  https://docs.unity3d.com/Manual/UnityEvents.html
- *Unity - Scripting API Documentation:*
  https://docs.unity3d.com/ScriptReference/
- *Game Programming Patterns* by *Robert Nystrom:*
  http://gameprogrammingpatterns.com

16
Service Locator

The Service Locator is a very straightforward pattern, and its name implies perfectly its purpose, which is locating services. In game development, services are usually game-mechanics-related systems that provide specific functionality—for example: spawners, save states, and online connectivity. Because games are mainly composed of layers of in-game systems communicating, functioning, and synchronizing with one another to simulate an interactive experience, the Service Locator creates a large number of dependencies between system components.

So, having a way for services to find one another through a central locator can streamline communication between components, while avoiding explicit references to the location of dependencies that a system might need to be able to run correctly. And that's what the Service Locator pattern offers: a global access point and registry to the core services of a program.

In this chapter, we will cover the following topics:

- The basics of the Service Locator pattern
- Implementing a global service locator that will act as a runtime linker

Technical requirements

The following chapter is hands on, so you will need to have a basic understanding of Unity and C#.

We will be using the following Unity-specific engine and C# language concepts:

- Generics
- Singleton

If you are unfamiliar with these concepts, please review Chapter 6, *Singleton*.

The code files of this chapter can be found on GitHub:

```
https://github.com/PacktPublishing/Hands-On-Game-Development-Patterns-with-
Unity-2018
```

Check out the following video to see the code in action:

```
http://bit.ly/2U8Mb6H
```

An overview of the Service Locator

The Service Locator is a straightforward pattern and doesn't have much academic theory behind it, so we can safely say it falls into the category of pragmatic patterns. As its name implies, it locates services for a client; it achieves this by maintaining a central registry of classes that offer specific services. This registry can be updated dynamically at runtime by having services register themselves when available.

Another common component of the Service Locator is its local cache, which uses the same principles as the Object Pool. A Service Locator might hold instances of its most-requested services in memory to avoid using too much memory.

Let's review a diagram of a typical Service Locator implementation:

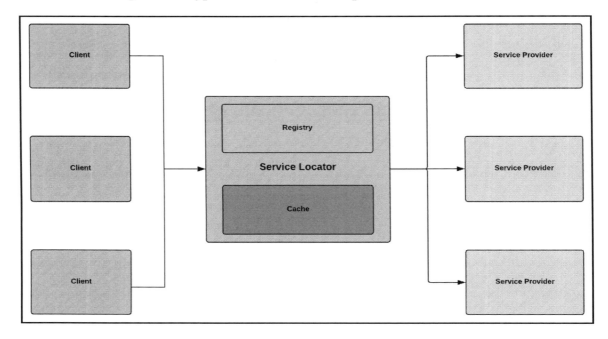

As we can see, we could easily say that the **Service Locator** is acting like a proxy between the clients (requestors) and the service providers, and this means that the relationship between both is a decoupled one. A client will only need to call the **Service Locator** when it has a dependency to resolve.

 It's important to remember that the software architecture term *client* is often used to describe a class using the functionalities of another class, or other classes—it has nothing to do with the end user of an application. Systems can be clients of other systems without any human input.

Benefits and drawbacks

The Service Locator is a young pattern; its reputation in the industry is quite limited compared to more traditional patterns.

The following are the benefits of using the Service Locator:

- **Runtime optimization**: A Service Locator can optimize an application at runtime by dynamically detecting better libraries or components to use, depending on the context.
- **Contextual run-time locators**: It's possible to have multiple Service Locators in memory, each configured for a specific runtime context, such as testing, staging, and production.
- **Simpler than Dependency Injection**: A Service Locator is simpler to implement than a **Dependency Injection** (DI)-driven architecture, mainly because it's a centralized approach to managing dependencies.

The following are the drawbacks of using the Service Locator:

- **Blackboxing**: Services contained in the registry can become invisible to other components in a system. This approach can make it harder to detect errors or regressions.
- **Security hole**: Depending on the overall architecture of the code base, the Service Locator could permit the injection code that could exploit your systems.
- **Globally accessible**: If implemented as a Singleton, the Service Locator can suffer from the same issues of globally accessible managers and components, making them harder to unit test.

Use case example

Our use case will be straightforward, and we will not focus on a specific in-game system. Instead, we will concentrate on building a simple Service Locator that will offer the ability to *link* a client to the following services dynamically:

- **Currency converter**: A service that converts in-game currency to a real-world value
- **Lighting coordinator**: A system that manages the lights in our scenes
- **Lobby coordinator**: A service that coordinates with the multiplayer lobby to set up "death matches"

But, of course, we could add many available services to the registry, but for this example, we will focus on just those three.

Code example

As we are going to see from the following code example, implementing a basic Service Locator is a straightforward process:

1. Let's start by implementing the most important ingredient: the `ServiceLocator` class:

```
using System;
using System.Collections.Generic;

public class ServiceLocator : Singleton<ServiceLocator>
{
    private IDictionary<object, object> m_Services;

    public override void Awake()
    {
        base.Awake();
        FillRegistry();
    }

    private void FillRegistry()
    {
        m_Services = new Dictionary<object, object>();

        m_Services.Add(typeof(LobbyCoordinator), new
        LobbyCoordinator());
        m_Services.Add(typeof(CurrencyConverter), new
        CurrencyConverter());
```

```
        m_Services.Add(typeof(LightingCoordinator), new
        LightingCoordinator());
    }

    public T GetService<T>()
    {
        try
        {
            return (T)m_Services[typeof(T)];
        }
        catch
        {
            throw new ApplicationException("The requested service
is not found.");
        }
    }
}
```

2. This version of a Service Locator has two primary responsibilities:
   - Managing the registry with the `FillRegistry()` function
   - Returning a specified service to the client with the `GetService(T)` function

Those two functions refer to the central registry that's in the form of a `Dictionary`. Of course, we could separate these responsibilities into individual classes, instead of encapsulating them inside local functions, but for this example, we are keeping it simple.

Now that we have our Service Locator set up, we can now start implementing some services for our clients.

3. Our first service is `Currencyconverter`; this is essential for modern games when we consider that they usually include an in-game purchase and lootbox mechanics:

```
using UnityEngine;

public class CurrencyConverter
{
    public void ConvertToUsDollar(int inGameCurrency)
    {
        Debug.Log("Players in-game currency is worth 100$ US");
    }
}
```

4. Our second service is `LightingCoordinator`; it's responsible for managing all the lights in our scenes:

```
using UnityEngine;

public class LightingCoordinator
{
    public void TurnOffLights()
    {
        Debug.Log("Turning off all the lights.");
    }
}
```

5. Our last service is `LobbyCoordinator`; this is responsible for making sure that our player can join an active lobby when required:

```
using UnityEngine;

public class LobbyCoordinator
{
    public void AddPlayerToLobby()
    {
        Debug.Log("Adding a player to the lobby.");
    }
}
```

We now have three services, each with specific responsibilities, available to our clients if need be. But we have an apparent limitation: at the moment, we are adding services to the central registry only by hand, and this is, of course, not the best approach for production code; however, it is acceptable for us to test our first pass implementation of a Service Locator. Later on, as a practical exercise, it would be wise to add the option for service providers to register themselves dynamically into the service registry:

```
// TODO: We need to be able to fill the registry dynamically.
private void FillRegistry()
{
    m_Services = new Dictionary<object, object>();
    m_Services.Add(typeof(LobbyCoordinator), new
    LobbyCoordinator());
    m_Services.Add(typeof(CurrencyConverter), new
    CurrencyConverter());
    m_Services.Add(typeof(LightingCoordinator), new
    LightingCoordinator());
}
```

6. And now, for our final class, we are going to implement the client:

```
using UnityEngine;

public class ClientServiceLocator : MonoBehaviour
{
    void Update()
    {
        if (Input.GetKeyDown("o"))
        {
            ServiceLocator.Instance.GetService<LightingCoordinator>
            ().TurnOffLights();
        }

        if (Input.GetKeyDown("c"))
        {
            ServiceLocator.Instance.GetService<CurrencyConverter>
            ().ConvertToUsDollar(10);
        }

        if (Input.GetKeyDown("l"))
        {
            ServiceLocator.Instance.GetService<LobbyCoordinator>
            ().AddPlayerToLobby();
        }
    }
}
```

Once we have implemented the client-side code, we can appreciate the benefits of the Service Locator. We are now able to have access to any core service of our code base without having to know the location of its class or how to initialize it. We have a global but straightforward interface that we can query from anywhere that dynamically links a client with a service while decoupling the entire process of localizing a service and initializing it.

Summary

In this chapter, we reviewed the Service Locator, a pattern that is a global solution that can resolve the recurring challenge of managing dependencies between objects that rely on services (functionalities) that other objects offer. In its simplest form, the Service Locator decouples the relationship between a client (requester) and a service provider. But in its most advanced form, it can also optimize memory usage if extended with a local cache that will reuse instances of providers when required.

In the next chapter, we will explore the DI pattern, which we could say is somewhat the opposite of the Service Locator in its approach but has a similar intent.

Exercise

In the code example, we implemented a simple version of the Service Locator so we could have a clear overview of its core intent and design. But for an exercise, I would recommend you take this basic draft of the Service Locator and expand it into something that could be production ready, by doing the following:

- Encapsulate the registry and cache components into self-contained classes.
- Implement the cache with a combination of the Factory and Prototype patterns.
- Implement the ability for services to add themselves dynamically to the registry.
- Write a standard interface for your service providers so you can effectively manage them.

 It's good practice to approach design patterns like a jazz musician approaches a melody. Once you understand the core theme of a pattern, extend it, improvise on it, and make it your own, while staying accurate to its fundamental design.

Further reading

Inversion of Control Containers and the Dependency Injection pattern, by Martin Fowler (https://martinfowler.com/articles/injection.html#UsingAServiceLocator)

17
Dependency Injection

I was introduced to the **Dependency Injection (DI)** pattern when I was working as a web developer, and I've been using it for years. However, I have noticed that DI is not well-known in the gaming industry. I suspect this is because it's a pattern that was developed to resolve design issues in business-oriented applications, and not for high-performance software such as video games.

As its names implies, DI is about injecting dependencies; it might sound abstract at first, but it's a quite simple concept. Classes often need instances of other classes to complete specific functions. So instead of having a class initialize its own dependencies, we inject them through its constructor or a parameter in one of its functions. This approach decouples the explicit relationships between classes, and it makes it easier to test our code, because we can easily inject mock objects that execute unit tests.

As you will see in this book, DI has its limitations, and it is not necessarily compatible with Unity's programming environment. This will become especially clear when you start to introduce more advanced versions of DI, in the form of **Inversion of Control (IoC)** containers.

The following topics will be covered in this chapter:

- We will review the fundamentals of the DI pattern
- We will explore the core concepts behind IoC containers and how they relate to DI
- We will resolve a dependency issue prompted by the implementation of a feature that permits customizing the initial configurations of a superbike for a racing game

Technical requirements

The following chapter is hands-on; you will need to have a basic understanding of Unity and C#.

We will be using the following specific Unity engine and C# language concepts:

- Interfaces
- Constructors

If you are unfamiliar with these concepts, please review them before moving forward.

The code files from this chapter can be found on GitHub:

`https://github.com/PacktPublishing/Hands-On-Game-Development-Patterns-with-Unity-2018`

Check out the following video to see the code in action:

`http://bit.ly/2Oww7WM`

An overview of Dependency Injection

As its name implies, the DI pattern's core purpose is to inject dependencies into the classes that need them. There are three ways to achieving this with DI, as follows:

- **Constructor injection**: We inject dependencies through a class's constructor.
- **Setter injection**: We inject dependencies through a class's function parameters.
- **Interface injection**: The dependency's interface offers an injector method to pass a dependency to a client.

In this chapter, we will only review the constructor and setter techniques, because they are the most common.

Dependencies are usually classes that offer a particular service that other classes can utilize to complete specific functions. A classic example is a manager class that is responsible for establishing a connection to a database to execute queries. To fulfill this responsibility, the database manager is dependent on vendor-specific classes that act as interfaces to certain types of databases.

To avoid having the database manager retrieve and initialize a specific dependency every time it needs to connect to a particular type of database, we could provide them by injecting them when needed. In other words, we are decoupling the relationship between the dependent and its dependencies.

A UML diagram is not the best tool to describe the purposes of a DI pattern, but let's review a simplified diagram that outlines what we are going to implement as our use case:

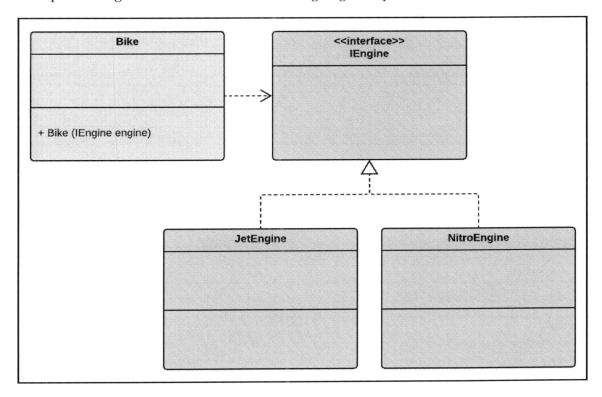

The case presented in the preceding diagram is similar to the database manager example that we just examined. We have a class named `Bike` that needs an engine to run correctly. Instead of having the `Bike` class initialize a specific type of engine depending on a particular condition, we made it accept a parameter of the `IEngine` type in its constructor. With this approach, we can have `Bike` receive any concrete class that implements `IEngine`, like in this example, with `JetEngine` and `NitroEngine`.

This arrangement provides us with a lot of extensibility; we could write dozens of different types of engines, each with their particular features, and the `Bike` would be able to accept them without any modification to its current structure.

But of course, DI is not without its drawbacks, as you are going to see in the next section.

DI follows the core principals of IoC, which is about inverting the flow control of a system. In the case of DI, it's about inverting the process of dependency management. Another pattern that follows IoC principals is the service locator, which you can review in `Chapter 16`, *Service Locator*.

Benefits and drawbacks

Like the Singleton pattern, the DI pattern is somewhat controversial, and its actual benefits and drawbacks are often contested. I suspect this is because its design is straightforward and programmers tend to be cautious of anything that looks too simple, because it's usually too good to be true.

The benefits are as follows:

- **Loose coupling**: Having classes receive instances to dependencies instead of explicitly initializing them can reduce tight coupling in a code base.
- **Testable code**: DI makes it easier to run tests by making it possible to inject mock objects that can run specific scenarios.
- **Concurrent development**: DI offers a way to decouple objects and enforce communication through interfaces. This approach makes it easier for a team of programmers to write classes that utilize each other.

The drawbacks are as follows:

- **Disputes**: DI is a type of pattern that causes a lot of debates in a team, because the best approach is not always clear, especially when a more advanced form of DI is considered, such as the use of IoC injection containers.
- **Framework dependency**: The basic form of DI is very limited; once a certain degree of complexity is achieved, it becomes necessary to implement a third-party IoC framework to manage the injection of dependencies in a configurable manner. As a consequence, the code base often becomes dependent on the framework and cannot be easily removed.
- **Ravioli code**: Overzealous use of DI and related best practices can result in a code base that's overly encapsulated and broken up into too many individual classes, making it difficult to understand.

To test a candidate's ability to debate technical subject matters, interviewers often ask a candidate to give an opinion on a controversial pattern, such as DI and Singleton. It's a good practice, as an interviewee, to showcase a balanced view on any issue by taking into account the benefits and drawbacks.

Use case example

Let's suppose that we are working on a racing game set in the future, with superbikes. We have to implement a feature quickly, in which a player can customize their bike by choosing an engine and driver from a list of available options before starting a race. In other words, our bike object has two specific dependencies: an engine and a driver. Using the DI pattern, we are going to manage these dependencies without adding unnecessary complexity to our code base.

First, we are going to look at the incorrect way to manage dependencies in a class so that you can understand the benefits of DI in contrast to the opposite approach.

The wrong way, without DI

Before going into the implementation phase of our use case, let's first review an example of a class that uses an ill-considered way of initializing and managing its dependencies:

```
using UnityEngine;

public class Bike : MonoBehaviour
{
    public enum EngineType
    {
        Jet,
        Turbo,
        Nitro
    };

    public enum DriverType
    {
        Human,
        Android
    };

    private Engine m_Engine;
    private Driver m_Driver;

    public void SetEngine(EngineType type)
    {
        switch (type)
        {
            case EngineType.Jet:
                m_Engine = new JetEngine();
                break;
            case EngineType.Turbo:
```

```
            m_Engine = new TurboEngine();
        case EngineType.Nitro:
            m_Engine = new NitroEngine();
    }

    Debug.Log("The bike is running with the engine: " + m_Engine);
}

public void SetDriver(DriverType type)
{
    switch (type)
    {
        case DriverType.Human:
            m_Driver = new HumanDriver();
            break;
        case DriverType.Android:
            m_Driver = new AndroidDriver();
    }

    Debug.Log("The driver of the bike is a: " + driver);
}

public void StartEngine()
{
    if (m_Engine != null)
    {
        // Start the bike's engine
        m_Engine.Start();
        // Give control of the bike to the driver
        m_Driver.Control(this);
    }
}
}
```

At first glance, this might seem like a reasonable approach, but let's imagine that we are working in a team of game programmers and each is implementing new types of engine behaviors. If we want our `Bike` class to support them, we will need to modify the `EngineType` enum and also update the `switch` case inside the body of the `SetEgnine()` method. This approach can become very bothersome over time if multiple programmers are working on the class at the same time.

We are having the same issue with the `SetDriver()` function; with this arrangement, adding new types of drivers will become a choir and will probably be prone to errors. So let's implement the same class in a step-by-step approach by using DI as our foundation.

The right way with DI

The implementation of DI is quite straightforward, and that's probably its main benefit. So, this section should be painless:

1. Let's start by writing our `Bike` class; we could say that it's the actual client in this DI pattern example, mainly because it's the class that's dependent on receiving dependencies during the injection process:

```
using UnityEngine;

public class Bike : MonoBehaviour
{
    private IEngine m_Engine;
    private IDriver m_Driver;

    // Setter injection
    public void SetEngine(IEngine engine)
    {
        m_Engine = engine;
    }
    // Setter injection
    public void SetDriver(IDriver driver)
    {
        m_Driver = driver;
    }

    public void StartEngine()
    {
        // Starting the engine
        m_Engine.StartEngine();
        // Giving control of the bike to a driver (AI or player)
        m_Driver.Control(this);
    }

    public void TurnLeft()
    {
        Debug.Log("The bike is turning left");
    }

    public void TurnRight()
    {
        Debug.Log("The bike is turning right");
    }
}
```

As you can see, the `SetEngine()` and `SetDriver()` functions are not aware of what specific engine or driver they are receiving—only that they expect a generic type of them. In other words, the `Bike` class is no longer responsible for the initialization process of its dependencies. This approach is very flexible; we could write an infinite number of engine classes, each with their own specific behaviors, and if we stayed consistent with the implementation contract of the `IEngine` interface, we wouldn't need to modify the `Bike` class directly for it to be suitable to use new engines.

You will also notice that this approach is likewise valid for the `driver` dependency. The `Bike` doesn't need to know who the driver is; it just needs to know that the entity that's taking control implemented the `IDriver` interface so that they could communicate with each other.

For testing purposes, this flexibility is helpful; we could easily inject mock `engine` or `driver` objects at runtime and run some automated unit tests on the `Bike` implementations.

2. Now, let's write the interfaces for our two primary types of dependencies: engines and drivers:

  - The `IEngine` interface is as follows:

    ```
    public interface IEngine
    {
        void StartEngine();
    }
    ```

  - The `IDriver` interface is as follows:

    ```
    public interface IDriver
    {
        void Control(Bike bike);
    }
    ```

3. In the following step, we are going to write all of our concrete classes for each primary type of component that our bike needs to function correctly:

  - The `JetEngine` class is as follows:

    ```
    using UnityEngine;

    public class JetEngine : IEngine
    {
        public void StartEngine()
    ```

```
    {
        ActivateJetStream();
        Debug.Log("Engine started");
    }

    private void ActivateJetStream()
    {
        Debug.Log("The jet stream is activated");
    }
}
```

- The `NitroEngine` class is as follows:

```
using UnityEngine;

public class NitroEngine : IEngine
{
    public void StartEngine()
    {
        OpenNitroValve();
        Debug.Log("Engine started");
    }

    private void OpenNitroValve()
    {
        Debug.Log("The nitro valve is open");
    }
}
```

It's important to note that each engine encapsulates its internal mechanism while staying consistent with the implementation of the `IEngine` interface. It's this consistent approach that permits DI.

- The `HumanDriver` class is as follows:

```
using UnityEngine;

public class HumanDriver : IDriver
{
    private Bike m_Bike;

    public void Control(Bike bike)
    {
        m_Bike = bike;
        Debug.Log("A human (player) will control the bike");
    }
}
```

- The `AndroidDriver` class is as follows:

```
using UnityEngine;

public class AndroidDriver : IDriver
{
    private Bike m_Bike;

    public void Control(Bike bike)
    {
        m_Bike = bike;
        Debug.Log("This bike will be controlled by an AI");
    }
}
```

The `HumanDriver` class is intended to give control of the `Bike` to a player, which we will do in the upcoming `Client` class. The `AndroidDriver` class is meant to support an AI entity that could drive the `Bike` and act as a rival to the player during a race.

4. Finally, our `Client` class, which we will use to test our system, is as follows:

```
using UnityEngine;

namespace Pattern.DependencyInjection
{
    public class Client : MonoBehaviour
    {
        // Bike controlled by the player
        public Bike m_PlayerBike;

        // Bike controlled by an android (AI)
        public Bike m_AndroidBike;

        void Awake()
        {
            // Set up a bike with a human driver and jet engine
            IEngine jetEngine = new JetEngine();
            IDriver humanDriver = new HumanDriver();

            m_PlayerBike.SetEngine(jetEngine);
            m_PlayerBike.SetDriver(humanDriver);
            m_PlayerBike.StartEngine();

            // Set up a bike with a AI driver and a nitro engine
            IEngine nitroEngine = new NitroEngine();
            IDriver androidDriver = new AndroidDriver();
```

```
                m_PlayerBike.SetEngine(jetEngine);
                m_PlayerBike.SetDriver(humanDriver);
                m_PlayerBike.StartEngine();
        }

        void Update()
        {
            if (Input.GetKeyDown(KeyCode.A))
            {
                m_PlayerBike.TurnLeft();
            }

            if (Input.GetKeyDown(KeyCode.D))
            {
                m_PlayerBike.TurnRight();
            }
        }

        void OnGUI()
        {
            GUI.color = Color.black;
            GUI.Label(new Rect(10, 10, 500, 20), "Press A to turn
LEFT and D to turn RIGHT");
            GUI.Label(new Rect(10, 30, 500, 20), "Output displayed
in the debug console");
        }
    }
}
```

Our `Client` class is quite straightforward; in the `Awake()` function, we inject the dependencies into two instances of a `Bike` class: `m_PlayerBike` and `m_AndroidBike`. In the `Update()` function, we listen for a player's input that permits them to control the `m_PlayerBike` instance.

This might look very straightforward and too simple to be true, but this pattern offers a lot of extensibility and flexibility, with little complexity, if used in moderation. In the next section, we are going to review a more advanced form of DI, which uses IoC containers.

 You may have noticed that we didn't use constructor injection in our code example; it's because we were working with a `MonoBehaviour` class, and we don't have access to its constructor. Some Unity developers do use the `Awake()` function to inject dependencies during the initialization process.

DI with IoC containers

IoC containers usually come in the form of frameworks; their primary responsibilities are to automate the DI process and manage the life space of dependencies. Before we start, it's important to note that most IoC containers are not designed to be compatible with Unity's coding model, and I don't recommend using them. On the other hand, it's important to be aware that they exist.

As we mentioned at the beginning of this chapter, DI is a handy and straightforward pattern, but it has its limitations. In the code example that we just implemented, we managed the injection of two dependencies at once, but imagine if we had dozens of them spread out over multiple classes. In that type of context, DI can become a choke point in your architecture. That is when IoC containers become useful, because they can automate the process of managing all of those injections.

The following is a quick summary of the functions that most IoC containers offer:

- **Registration**: The container offers a way to register dependencies and map them to the dependents correctly.
- **Resolving**: The container takes the responsibility of resolving the dependencies by initializing and injecting them.
- **Disposing**: The container will manage the lifespan of objects, including disposing them once they are not needed anymore.

The goal of this quick review of the IoC containers is not to debate whether they are necessary, but to become aware that the simple version of the DI pattern has its limitations. Once we have reached a certain degree of complexity and density with regard to the dependencies to inject, we need to consider implement or integrating an IoC container framework to manage the process.

Always be cautious about making your code base dependent on third-party frameworks; you might find yourself falling into the vendor lock-in anti-pattern, which I will describe in more detail in the final chapter of this book.

Summary

In this chapter, we reviewed the DI pattern, a simple pattern that has grown in popularity over the years. Its fame is explainable by the fact that it resolves a common challenge that every programmer faces daily, which is the management of dependencies between classes. In other words, it's a powerful tool to have in your toolkit, as long as you don't abuse it.

In the next chapter, we will explore the object pool pattern, another handy tool that is very popular with mobile game programmers.

Practical exercise

As a practical exercise, I recommend writing an application in C# using a popular IoC container framework. Because most of them are incompatible with the Unity engine, I suggest going native and coding a simple Windows application in Visual Studio.

In the *Further reading* section, I have added a list of popular IoC container frameworks.

Further reading

Some books that may be used as reference are as follows:

- *Dependency Injection in .NET* by Mark Seemann: `https://www.manning.com/books/dependency-injection-in-dot-net`
- *Dependency Injection Principles, Practices, and Patterns* by Steven van Deursen and Mark Seemann: `https://www.manning.com/books/dependency-injection-principles-practices-patterns`

Some IoC frameworks to consider are as follows:

- Ninject: `http://www.ninject.org`
- Castle Windsor: `https://github.com/castleproject/Windsor`

Section 7: Optimization Patterns

It's by mastering optimization that programmers in the gaming industry prove themselves and gain mastery. Unity might come *pre-optimized* on certain aspects, but it can be a trap because performance issues are often subtle and only appear after deploying on your target platform. So, getting into the habit of implementing the right design patterns early on in the production process might save you from having to crunch for long hours just before launch day.

The following chapters are included in this section:

- Chapter 18, *Object Pool*
- Chapter 19, *Spatial Partition*

Object Pool 18

The Object Pool pattern is straightforward to understand; as its name suggests, it organizes a pool of objects. The simplest way to visualize the design intent behind this pattern is to imagine a swimming pool filled to the brim with balloons of various colors. If you wish, you can take all the green ones out, play with them and, once done, put them back. In other words, you always have a collection of specific types of objects ready to be used, and a place to store them afterward.

If we translate this concept into code, what we have is specific types of objects already contained in memory, which we can pull from when we need and then pool them back into memory when we are finished. This approach means we are using a constant size of reserved memory for specific types of ready-made objects. As you may already presume, this is a very optimized way of managing objects for a video game project.

The following topics will be covered in this chapter:

- We will review the basics of the Object Pool pattern
- We will implement the Object Pool pattern to manage reusable game objects for a zombie game

Technical requirements

This chapter is hands-on; you will need to have a basic understanding of Unity and C#.

We will be using the following specific Unity engine and C# language concepts:

- Prefabs
- Singletons
- Namespaces

If you are unfamiliar with these concepts, please review them before starting this chapter.

The code files of this chapter can be found on GitHub:

`https://github.com/PacktPublishing/Hands-On-Game-Development-Patterns-with-Unity-2018`

Check out the following video to see the code in action:

`http://bit.ly/2WutcB2`

An overview of the Object Pool pattern

The Object Pool pattern is usually defined as a creational design pattern in academic documentation, but in this book, we have categorized it as an optimization pattern, because its core purpose is more aligned with optimization than the creation process – at least in the way we are going to use it.

The core concept of this pattern is simple; a pool in the form of a container holds a collection of initialized objects. Clients can request the Object Pool for a specific type and number of objects. The Client must return the objects to the Object Pool once it's done using them. So, this means the pool always get filled back up, and is never drained.

The following diagram illustrates the back and forth between the `Client` and the `ObjectPool`:

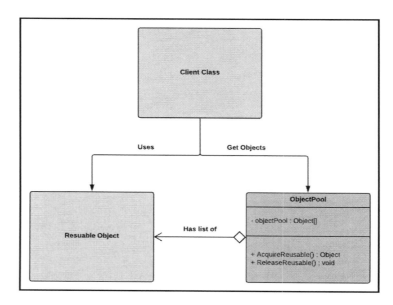

As you can see, the `Reusable Object` is always in memory; it is just its owner that switches between the Client and `ObjectPool`, depending on whether it's in an acquired or released state.

Benefits and drawbacks

The Object Pool pattern is quite popular with Unity developers, but it has its critics in the broader software development community:

Benefits:

- **Predictable memory usage**: Because the Object Pool pattern is configurable, you can set limits for the number of instances of specific objects available.
- **Performance boost**: By having objects already initialized in memory, you avoid the loading cost of initializing new ones.

Drawbacks:

- **Layering on already-managed memory**: Some criticize the Object Pool pattern as being unnecessary in most cases, because modern managed programming languages such as C# already optimally control memory allocation.
- **Unpredictable object states**: The main pitfall of the Object Pool pattern is that, if incorrectly managed, objects will be returned to the pool in their current state instead of their default one. This issue can cause unpredictable behaviors the next time they are pulled out of the pool, because objects might be in an unexpected state.

 Object pools have a lot of added value for mobile games, because phones have limited memory and resources compared to the average PC or console.

Use case example

As with the other creational patterns, the Object Pool can be a great pattern to use when designing a spawn system. But, this time, we will focus on having a Client pulling and pooling directly from an Object Pool without any layers of abstraction between them, so we can see the system at work.

Just to give some context to the following code example, let's imagine we are doing a *Plants versus Zombies* clone. Like most zombie games, we have hordes of zombies moving toward a target. Each horde can contain various types of zombies, such as the following:

- Walkers
- Runners

But, what's important to consider is that every time our player kills one of them, instead of destroying the instance of the defeated zombie in memory, we can instead send it back to an Object Pool so that it can be used again afterward. With this approach, we are recycling our zombie-type entities instead of initializing new ones.

In the next section, we will implement this use case and adapt it, so that it works with Unity's GameObjects.

Code example

This chapter might be difficult to follow just by reading the code, because we are managing prefabs inside a scene. So, we recommend that you download the Unity project associated with this book on our Git depot at `https://github.com/PacktPublishing/Hands-On-Game-Development-Patterns-with-Unity-2018`.

In the Unity project, there should be a folder named Object Pool, with a scene included that will have the entire set of dependencies to run this example properly.

But, in case the GitHub address is unavailable, here's a quick list of steps that need to be done in order to execute the following code example inside a Unity scene:

1. Open a new scene, add an empty `GameObject`, and name it `Object Pool`.
2. Create a set of prefabs and related scripts for each type of zombie. Here are some examples of zombie behavior scripts:

    - Runner:

```
using UnityEngine;

namespace Zombie
{
    public class Runner : MonoBehaviour
    {
        public void Run()
        {
            // Zombie runs!
```

```
            }
        }
    }
```

- Walker:

```
using UnityEngine;

namespace Zombie
{
    public class Walk: MonoBehaviour
    {
        public void Walk()
        {
            // Zombie walks!
        }
    }
}
```

- Screamer:

```
using UnityEngine;

namespace Zombie
{
    public class Screamer : MonoBehaviour
    {
        public void Scream()
        {
            // Zombie screams!
        }
    }
}
```

3. Attach the `ObjectPool` script to the `GameObject` **Object Pool**.

4. In the inspector of the `GameObject` Object Pool, configure the list of zombie prefabs that the `ObjectPool` instance will manage. You can refer to the following screenshot for reference:

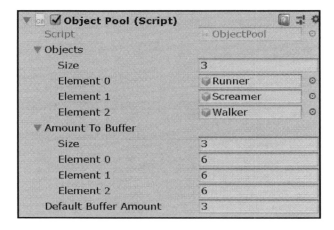

Now, it's time for us to write the `ObjectPool` class. As you will see, it's quite long, so it's essential we read through it, and review its core features afterward:

```csharp
using UnityEngine;
using System.Collections.Generic;

public class ObjectPool : Singleton<ObjectPool>
{
        // The objects to pool.
        public GameObject[] objects;

        // The list of pooled objects.
        public List<GameObject>[] pooledObjects;

        // The amount of objects to buffer.
        public int[] amountToBuffer;

        public int defaultBufferAmount = 3;

        // The container of pooled objects.
        protected GameObject containerObject;

        void Start()
        {
            containerObject = new GameObject("ObjectPool");
            pooledObjects = new List<GameObject>[objects.Length];
```

```
        int i = 0;
        foreach (GameObject obj in objects)
        {
            pooledObjects[i] = new List<GameObject>();

            int bufferAmount;

            if (i < amountToBuffer.Length)
            {
                bufferAmount = amountToBuffer[i];
            }
            else
            {
                bufferAmount = defaultBufferAmount;
            }

            for (int n = 0; n < bufferAmount; n++)
            {
                GameObject newObj = Instantiate(obj) as GameObject;
                newObj.name = obj.name;
                PoolObject(newObj);
            }

            i++;
        }
    }

    // Pull an object of a specific type from the pool.
    public GameObject PullObject(string objectType)
    {
        bool onlyPooled = false;
        for (int i = 0; i < objects.Length; i++)
        {
            GameObject prefab = objects[i];

            if (prefab.name == objectType)
            {
                if (pooledObjects[i].Count > 0)
                {
                    GameObject pooledObject = pooledObjects[i][0];
                    pooledObject.SetActive(true);
                    pooledObject.transform.parent = null;

                    pooledObjects[i].Remove(pooledObject);

                    return pooledObject;
                }
                else if (!onlyPooled)
```

```
                        {
                            return Instantiate(objects[i]) as GameObject;
                        }

                        break;
                    }
                }

                // Null if there's a hit miss.
                return null;
            }

            // Add object of a specific type to the pool.
            public void PoolObject(GameObject obj)
            {
                for (int i = 0; i < objects.Length; i++)
                {
                    if (objects[i].name == obj.name)
                    {
                        obj.SetActive(false);
                        obj.transform.parent = containerObject.transform;
                        pooledObjects[i].Add(obj);
                        return;
                    }
                }

                Destroy(obj);
            }
        }
```

So, here's a quick breakdown of what's happening in the ObjectPool class in each function:

- Start(): In this function, we are initializing a list() that will contain instances of our pooled objects.
- PullObject(): By calling this function, Clients can request an instance of an object from the pool just by specifying the name of its type. If we have it in store, we return its instance; if not, we initialize a new instance of it.
- PoolObject(): A client can use this function to return instances of objects to the pool. ObjectPool will deactivate the returning object and attach it back to itself as a child, so it can keep it contained.

We can also see that our ObjectPool class is a singleton; this is a common approach, because we usually need to have Object Pools globally accessible and always available. To learn how to implement a singleton, please review Chapter 6, *Singleton*.

The next step is to test out our `ObjectPool` with a `Client` class:

```
using UnityEngine;

public class Client : MonoBehaviour
{
    void Update()
    {
            if (Input.GetKeyDown(KeyCode.G))
            {
                GameObject walker =
ObjectPool.Instance.PullObject("Walker");
                walker.transform.Translate(Vector3.forward *
Random.Range(-5.0f, 5.0f));
                walker.transform.Translate(Vector3.right *
Random.Range(-5.0f, 5.0f));
            }

            if (Input.GetKeyDown(KeyCode.P))
            {
                object[] objs =
GameObject.FindObjectsOfType(typeof(GameObject));

                foreach (object o in objs)
                {
                    GameObject obj = (GameObject)o;

                    if (obj.gameObject.GetComponent<Zombie.Walker>() !=
null)
                    {
                        ObjectPool.Instance.PoolObject(obj);
                    }
                }
            }
        }
    }
```

Our `Client` class is quite straightforward:

- If the player presses *G*, we request an instance of a Walker zombie from the `ObjectPool`. Then, we place it randomly in the scene.

- If the player presses *P*, we send all the Walker objects that are currently in our scene back into the pool.

And that's it; with one class, we can implement a simple, configurable, and extensible Object Pool.

Summary

We have just added the Object Pool pattern to our toolkit; it's one of the most useful patterns for Unity developers because, as we saw in our code example, we can easily recycle GameObjects that are already in our scene without having to initialize new ones. When dealing with huge prefabs that contain a lot of data and components to initialize, this pattern can help you avoid inconsistent frame rates.

In the next chapter, we are going to explore the Spatial Partition pattern—a subject matter that's quite important to understand when building open-world games.

Exercise

Now that you have learned all the core creational patterns, such as Factory, Prototype, and Object Pool, it would be a valuable practical exercise to combine all those patterns and build the ultimate Spawn System. The goal is to have a system that reuses instances of objects of specific types and only creates new ones when it's necessary, and, if it does, uses a Factory.

Further reading

- *Game Programming Patterns* by Robert Nystrom
  `http://gameprogrammingpatterns.com`

19
Spatial Partition

In this chapter, we are going to review the Spatial Partition pattern; the concept of spatial partitioning is prevalent in computer graphics and is used for organizing the objects in a virtual space in an optimal way. This approach is also valid for the management of GameObjects placed inside of a Unity scene. By implementing the core principles of the Spatial Partition pattern, we can divide a large environment that's filled to the brim with two-dimensional or three-dimensional objects, and still be able to maintain a degree of consistent performance. As you will see in this chapter, this pattern is one of the core ingredients that make the production of large AAA open-world games possible.

The following topics will be covered in this chapter:

- We will review the basic principles behind the Spatial Partition pattern
- We will implement a mini game in which a predator hunts prey in a scene

Technical requirements

This chapter is hands-on, and you will need to have a basic understanding of Unity and C#.

We will be using the following specific Unity engine and C# language concept:

- LINQ

If you are unfamiliar with this concept, please review it before moving forward.

LINQ is a very powerful query language that's somewhat similar to SQL; it can be a time saver when you want to simply iterate through a data structure.

The code files from this chapter can be found on GitHub:

```
https://github.com/PacktPublishing/Hands-On-Game-Development-Patterns-with-
Unity-2018
```

Check out the following video to see the code in action:

```
http://bit.ly/2FAyWCf
```

An overview of the Spatial Partition pattern

Game programmers are often faced with the problem of finding a way to quickly locate the specific entities in a scene that are closest to a reference point, for example, the player character. In Unity, there are many approaches to solving this problem, such as the following:

- Implement a ray casting system that will scan the area around the player character and report the locations of specific entities.
- Use Unity's API features, such as the `GameObject.Find()` function, to locate specific entities in the scene, and then compare their coordinates to those of the player character.

The first option is valid, but if we have a complex three-dimensional environment, it might be difficult to locate all of the entities that we are looking for, because they might be behind other objects and cannot be intersected by the ray. The second option might not be ideal performance-wise, because we will need to iterate through a list that includes every entity in the scene until we find every instance of a specific type.

We can resolve this type of technical challenge by using the Spatial Partition pattern; it was designed for this purpose. One thing that we need to address first is the name of this pattern. The term **Spatial Partition** can be misleading: we are not organizing or modifying the virtual space that we are partitioning. We are doing the opposite; we are removing space from the equation.

We achieve this by putting three-dimensional objects that are in a scene into a flat data structure that efficiently represents, in the memory, the distance between those objects in relation to each other without having to do calculations on the exact coordinates. This approach permits us to do fast and straightforward calculations to find the entities that are the closest to or farthest from a reference point.

In other words, we are sub-dividing a virtual space into a structure that's easier to analyze. An example of a universal structure that's easy to represent in memory (and that is often used to divide space into individual containers) is a fixed grid. In the following diagram, you can see a visual representation of this concept. The grid contains squares, which we will call **cells**. Those cells include **units**. Those units can be anything—a specific type of enemy character or hidden loot boxes spread out across a vast map:

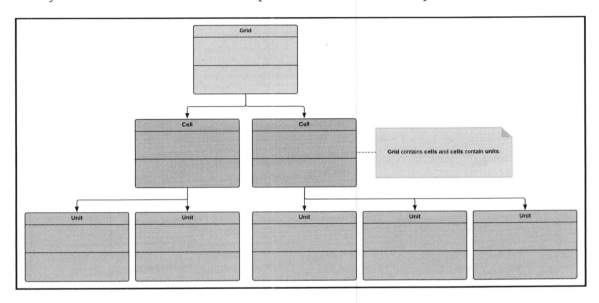

Now, let's imagine that this grid is superimposed on the enormous open-world map of an RPG video game. Each cell (square) represents a virtual 2x2 km area. We know that our player character has spawned in a specific cell (square) on the map, but we want to offer him the option to quickly travel to an area that's filled with level-2 monsters that he can fight. By using a Spatial Partition, we can easily calculate for the nearest entities of a specific type in the memory without having to scan the entire three-dimensional environment.

The results of the calculations can suggest to us a nearby cell (square) that contains the largest grouping of enemies of level 2. With this information, we can move our player character into a random position inside of the suggested cell (square), so that he can loot the area. As you will see in the next sections, Spatial Partitioning simplifies the process of managing entities that reside in complex two-dimensional and three-dimensional spaces.

Benefits and drawbacks

The drawbacks of this pattern are quite limited (and are non-existent in most cases) because it's so easy to use.

The benefits are as follows:

- **Reusable**: We can use the Spatial Partition pattern to optimize the way that we manage anything that's formed of entities spread out in two-dimensional or three-dimensional space (for example, user interfaces).
- **Simplification**: A Spatial Partition makes it easier to implement code that calculates spatial relationships between objects. It's very beneficial for those that are not good with math.

The drawbacks are as follows:

- **Not very dynamic**: Spatial Partitioning can lose all of its optimization benefits if you are trying to manage entities that are continually moving in space over an extended area. So, if you have a scene that's full of objects bouncing around at full speed, you will need to continuously update the data structure that contains the collection of entities and their grid positions. In that case, this process can be resource-intensive and not worth the effort.

The most important skill that a game programmer should acquire is mathematics. Being knowledgeable about design patterns is necessary to get into the industry, but it's not as important as a deep understanding of advanced mathematics.

Use case example

Imagine that we need to quickly prototype a straightforward mini game that simulates a non-player predator character hunting for prey on a map. The process of spawning the entities (prey and predator) in the environment is not complicated; actually, it is quite simple. However, how are we going to know if our predator is close to potential prey and move him toward it?

Consider the following possible solutions:

- We could query every object in the scene and compare their coordinates with those of the predator.
- We could implement a ray cast system that scans every object in the proximity of the predator, in order to spot potential prey.

These solutions could potentially work, but they could be burdensome to implement in a short time. However, with the Spatial Partition pattern, we can avoid this lengthy process by making sure that all the entities in our scene get contained in a data structure that organizes the prey and predator by their relative positions. As you will see in our code example, writing this implementation is quite fast and useful, especially when you are in a rush and want to sketch out some basic AI navigation behaviors in code.

Code example

The following code example might look very rudimentary, but it can easily be expanded to implement more complex use cases. In a way, it's a foundation that we will be able to build on:

1. Let's start by implementing the core element of our pattern, the `Grid`:

```csharp
using System;
using System.Linq;
using UnityEngine;

public class Grid: MonoBehaviour
{
    private int m_SquareSize;
    private int m_NumberOfSquares;

    public Grid(int squareSize, int numberOfSquares)
    {
        // The size can represent anything (meters, km)
        m_SquareSize = squareSize;

        // Squares permits to subdivide the grid granulary
        m_NumberOfSquares = numberOfSquares;
    }

    public void AddToRandomnPosition(IUnit unit)
    {
        unit.AddToGrid(UnityEngine.Random.Range(0,
m_NumberOfSquares));
```

```
        }

        public int FindClosest(IUnit referenceUnit, IUnit[] list)
        {
            if (list != null)
            {
                // Using LINQ queries
                var points = list.Select(a =>
a.GetGridPosition()).ToList();
                var nearest = points.OrderBy(x => Math.Abs(x -
referenceUnit.GetGridPosition())).First();
                return nearest;
            }
            else
            {
                throw new ArgumentException("Parameters cannot be
null", "list");
            }
        }
    }
```

The first thing that you should take note of is the `AddToRandomnPosition()` function, in which we are adding units to squares in the grid with a `Random.Range()` call. We are doing this for two reasons. We want to test our `Grid` implementation quickly, so we are simulating having the entities spread out in an environment at random positions. We also want to showcase how we can use Spatial Partitioning in combination with a spawn system to manage the spawning of entities within a specific optimized grid space. In other words, we can partition the virtual space of our scene in the memory, even before initializing the things that will inhabit it.

Another function to analyze is `FindClosest()`; note that we are using two LINQ queries. The first query extracts a list of grid positions from a list of units. With the second one, we are querying this list to find the nearest cell in relation to a reference unit. For those that have never worked with LINQ, it's a built-in C# query language that permits finding and extracting elements in a collection with a single line of code. It's an excellent tool to use when you need to prototype and quickly write implementations that use data structures and collections.

2. Now, we need a way for our units to register themselves into a specific cell of the `Grid`. Let's start by implementing an interface to manage our unit types:

```
public interface IUnit
{
    // The Unit can add itself to the grid
```

```
    void AddToGrid(int cell);

    // The Unit can return is current grid position
    int GetGridPosition();
}
```

It's quite a straightforward interface; the `GetGridPosition()` function returns the grid position of a `Unit`. A question that might arise is, why are we not implementing a function that will return the actual location of a `Unit` in the scene? It's because, in Unity, if a GameObject has a `Transform` component attached to it, we can directly ask this component to return its position inside of a three-dimensional scene. In other words, we are using Unity's API to do the heavy lifting for us.

3. We are going to implement two types of units for our code example; let's start with the `Prey`:

```
using UnityEngine;

public class Prey : MonoBehaviour, IUnit
{
    private int m_Square;

    public void AddToGrid(int square)
    {
        m_Square = square;
    }

    public int GetGridPosition()
    {
        return m_Square;
    }
}
```

4. Next up is our `Predator` class; he hunts our `Prey`:

```
using UnityEngine;

public class Predator : MonoBehaviour, IUnit
{
    private int m_Square;

    public void AddToGrid(int square)
    {
        m_Square = square;
    }
```

```
        public int GetGridPosition()
        {
            return m_Square;
        }
    }
```

We can see that both our `Predator` and `Prey` have two primary responsibilities, linking their positions into a specific cell of the grid and returning that cell number if requested.

5. Finally, our `Client` class, which we are using to spawn `Prey` on the `Grid` and unleash the `Predator` upon them, is as follows:

```
using UnityEngine;

namespace Pattern.SpatialPartition
{
    public class Client : MonoBehaviour
    {
        private Grid m_Grid;
        private IUnit[] m_Preys;

        void Start()
        {
            m_Grid = new Grid(4, 16);
            Debug.Log("Grid generated");
        }

        void Update()
        {
            if (Input.GetKeyDown(KeyCode.P))
            {
                IUnit prey;
                int numberOfPrey = 5;
                m_Preys = new IUnit[numberOfPrey];

                for (int i = 0; i < numberOfPrey; i++)
                {
                    prey = new Prey();
                    m_Grid.AddToRandomnPosition(prey);
                    m_Preys[i] = prey;

                    Debug.Log("A prey was spawned @ square: " +
m_Preys[i].GetGridPosition());
                }
            }
```

```
            if (Input.GetKeyDown(KeyCode.H))
            {
                IUnit predator;
                predator = new Predator();
                m_Grid.AddToRandomnPosition(predator);
                Debug.Log("A predator was spawned @ square: " +
predator.GetGridPosition());

                int closest = m_Grid.FindClosest(predator,
m_Preys);
                Debug.Log("The closest prey is @ square: " +
closest);
            }
        }

        void OnGUI()
        {
            GUI.color = Color.black;
            GUI.Label(new Rect(10, 10, 500, 20), "Press P to spawn
prey on the grid.");
            GUI.Label(new Rect(10, 30, 500, 20), "Press H to hunt
some prey.");
            GUI.Label(new Rect(10, 50, 500, 20), "Open Debug
Console to view the output.");
        }
    }
}
```

That's it; note that we never had to deal with the actual three-dimensional coordinates of objects to find their relative positions. We are avoiding a lot of unnecessary calculations by dividing the space into a grid and containing the objects within it. We are reducing the complexity by compartmentalizing it.

Of course, in our code example, we went with the easy route and avoided calculating the relative positions of our Units before adding them to a specific square in the Grid, but this can easily be added if need be. The most important takeaway is that we should always avoid doing complex calculations on the entities in a three-dimensional space if we can merely partition and manage them inside of a data structure that we can easily search and manipulate.

Summary

In this chapter, we took a simple approach to learning a pattern that offers a solution to a very complex problem, which is how to organize the objects in a space optimally. We now have a tool that we can use to build open-world games and a quick solution for prototyping a game in which grids are a central component (for example, a puzzle game).

In the final chapter of this book, we are going to review a subject that's the complete opposite of what we just explored: anti-patterns, the antithesis of design patterns.

Practice

In our code example, we implemented a straightforward use case of the Spatial Partition pattern. However, we limited ourselves to two-dimensional space; as a practical exercise, I would recommend expanding upon this basic example and organizing objects in a three-dimensional space. As inspiration, I would recommend observing the design of a Rubik's Cube. Note that it's composed of a collection of mini cubes; each can be considered a cell in a group.

Further reading

- *Mathematics for 3D Game Programming and Computer Graphics* by Eric Lengyel: https://www.mathfor3dgameprogramming.com

Section 8: Anti-Patterns in Unity

8

In this section, we are going to explore the dark side of design patterns by exposing their evil twin, Anti-Patterns. These negative patterns can be present in every level of your organization and can cause regressions in your code base in very subtle ways.

The following chapter is included in this section:

- Chapter 20, *The Anti-Patterns*

20
The Anti-Patterns

Throughout this book, we have reviewed best practices in software architecture by implementing various types of patterns. But what you might be asking yourself is if those patterns are so beneficial, why doesn't everyone use them? Or why do we still regularly see bug-ridden games coming out?

If current-day programmers have easy access to a wealth of information about software development best practices, it's reasonable to assume that there should be no reasons why we still have issues delivering stable video games and applications within reasonable deadlines. But in this chapter, we are going to explore why, in the software development industry, even extraordinarily competent and talented teams end up producing messy code and are unable to deliver a stable product.

In the previous chapters, we explored patterns that are designed to be beneficial and bring about positive results. But now, we are going to study their evil twins, in the form of Anti-Patterns. These destructive patterns are subtle; they don't always lurk in your code, but instead hurt you by causing fear, uncertainty, and doubt at every level of your organization. And that's why they are so difficult to recognize, as we are going to see in the following section.

The following topics will be covered in this chapter:

- We will be reviewing a list of common anti-patterns

The anti-patterns

There are probably over one hundred anti-patterns currently documented by experts in every field of software development. We won't be able to review them all in this chapter, but I have made a short list of those I found that are related to the misapplication of design patterns, either directly or indirectly. But I have also listed those that I've personally experienced in my career.

The academic research on the subject of anti-patterns is not thoroughly documented compared to established design patterns, so there are a lot of discrepancies in the naming of specific anti-patterns. As a result, a lot of the following material is my interpretation of prevalent anti-patterns and not official definitions. So, let's now dive into the subject matter and review some of the most relevant anti-patterns that I have experienced, and that I recommend to avoid.

False mastery

"If people knew how hard I worked to get my mastery, it wouldn't seem so wonderful at all."

- Michelangelo

What is it?
Programmers have access to a wealth of information, tools, and libraries that allow them to develop anything they want with ease. As a consequence, these advantages are making a lot of junior developers believe that they are masters of their craft when they are merely copying and pasting the work of others.

Why is it wrong?
Nothing obstructs your ability to learn more than believing that you already know everything. This dangerous mindset blinds you to your deficiencies and makes you unable to process feedback. As a result, you will never progress, and you will end up being a mediocre programmer for the rest of your career, even if you hold titles such as senior or technical director.

What is the root cause?
The leading cause of this premature disillusionment of mastery over your craft is that tools such as the Unity engine simplify the process of making games to the point that almost anyone can do it. But this means few understand what is happening under the hood of the engine in terms of the tools or programming language they are using.

So, by example, just because you can write a program in C# doesn't make you a C# expert, but knowing the intricacies of the language's libraries will make you into one.

How to avoid this?

The following is a list of professional habits that will help you avoid falling into the trap of this Anti-Pattern:

- Learn, learn, and never stop learning.
- Avoid hunting for titles such as senior, tech lead or CTO, and instead focus on gaining true mastery over your craft.
- Every time you use a new tool, library, and language, research as much as possible about its origins, as well as its intricacies.
- Humble yourself every day. Accept that you don't know everything and that it will take you several decades to become a true senior programmer.
- Teach, write a blog, and answer technical questions on forums. In other words, transfer the knowledge you know as well as absorbing new information. This approach will help you validate and structure your learning.

 Job titles given out in a start-up are not equivalent to those given in a large corporation. So don't be surprised when transitioning out from a small indie to a AAA studio that you end up back in a more junior role. The reason is simple: it's harder to gain seniority in a bigger team because you are competing with more programmers for better positions.

Fear of complexity

"Have no fear of perfection – you'll never reach it."

- Salvador Dali

What is it?
I personally have been the victim of this anti-pattern for years. It's the result of an overzealous belief that simplicity is always the best approach to code and, hence, you should avoid any solution that might look slightly more complex as the path of least resistance.

Why is it bad?
An irrational fear of complexity can prevent you from using sophisticated and advanced design patterns or algorithms to resolve issues. Thus, you reduce the potential for growth and limit your learning opportunities. Ultimately, it can prevent you from reaching maturity and seniority.

What is the root cause?
An earnest belief that the simplest solution is the best path to resolve any technical problem. But usually, it is an excuse to avoid doing research and leaving your comfort zone.

How to avoid?

Here are some questions that you should ask yourself every time you have to decide between an easy or complex solution to a problem:

- Am I currently feeling engaged in resolving a technical challenge or am I just trying to get things done?
- Am I afraid of looking stupid by suggesting a more advanced solution to a problem because I don't understand it?
- Does the simple solution I'm implementing scale with the overall architecture of the current code base overtime or does it just patch the problem?

So, in summary, always ask yourself this simple question when deciding between an easy or a complex solution to a problem: Are you choosing the most accessible approach because it's the right thing to do, or because you're just lazy and can't be bothered to adopt an advanced method that would require greater effort.

 You often hear programmers say that complexity causes more bugs. This is true but, to be more precise, it is unmanaged and misunderstood complexity that results in more bugs.

Too many managers

"We don't have as many managers as we should, but we would rather have too few than too many."

- Larry Page

What is it?
Managers are great; they offer a unique interface to a pool of complex sub-systems. Because video games are an extensive collection of systems that are constantly interacting with one another, having managers as interfaces can be very helpful in reducing dependencies.

Why is it wrong?

If every class is a manager, you end up with managers being dependent on other managers. In other words, managers become sub-systems of other managers until you find yourself in the same situation that you were trying to avoid, a spaghetti of dependencies. Another negative point is that managers are often implemented as singletons, which means that you have global dependencies spread throughout your code base.

The following is a code example that showcases a possible software architecture that's too dependent on Manager classes. If you see something similar in your source code, you might need to refactor your architecture:

```csharp
using UnityEngine;

public class GameManager : MonoBehaviour
{
    private Player m_Player;

    void Start()
    {
        // Get the player ID
        m_Player = PlayerManager.Instance.GetPlayer();
        // Sign-in to online services
        OnlineManager.Instance.LoginPlayer(m_Player);

        // Load save game data of the player
        SaveManager.Instance.LoadSaveGame(m_Player);

        // Load player preferred controller configuration
        IInputConfiguration inputConfig =
SaveManager.Instance.GetInputConfig(m_Player);
        InputManager.Instance.LoadControllerConfig(inputConfig);
    }
}
```

What is the root cause?

The root cause is usually inexperienced or lazy programmers who don't consider the overall architecture of their code base but instead focus on instant results.

How to avoid this?

Here's a list of good habits that might help you avoid this anti-pattern:

- Every time you are about to use a specific pattern, always consider using an alternative that might be more suitable. In other words, avoid defaulting to the easiest solution.

- Keep track of your architecture and the patterns that you are using. Raise a flag if you see too many classes with Manager in their title.
- If you are having issues implementing unit tests for your core systems, it's a good indication that there's something wrong in your architecture and it might be related to having too many singletons or classes that act like global Managers.

 New patterns, or permutations of established ones, are appearing regularly. It's good practice to keep an eye out for them by reading new books on the subject matter.

Ravioli code

"Organic architecture seeks superior sense of use and a finer sense of comfort, expressed in organic simplicity."

- Frank Lloyd Wright

What is it?
Ravioli code is the result of overzealous encapsulation and an architecture that's divided into too many individual classes.

Why is it wrong?
Most programmers have heard the term *Spaghetti code* during their career. It's often used to describe unstructured and messy code that's usually produced by junior programmers. But Ravioli code can be considered to be the opposite; it's often the result of overly designed code made by programmers who have a lot of experience but lack the desire to make their work readable to others.

In both cases, navigating and maintaining a code base suffering from those Anti-Patterns can become difficult.

What is the root cause?
A religious and dogmatic approach to programming and design patterns can make you write code that looks accurate but unreadable to others.

How to avoid this?
Here's some tips that might help you avoid this anti-pattern:

- Be willing to sacrifice accuracy for readability when necessary
- Always consider that design patterns do give you structure, but often at the sacrifice of readability
- Write code for an audience, and remember that those who might read it might not have the same skillset as you

Most professional programmers don't consciously use design patterns, often because they don't understand them or don't know how to implement them correctly. So, to be a great programmer, you have to be more aware than others of all the patterns that are available and how to use them properly.

Poltergeist

"Indeed, it is better to postpone, lest either we complete too little by hurrying, or wander too long in completing it."

- Tertullian

What is it?
Poltergeist objects are usually the result of code that was implemented to solve a temporary architecture issue, but that remained in the code base longer than it should have.

Why is it wrong?
The density of code that you have to maintain often relates to the frequency of bugs you might have to fix every time you make a change. Another side-effect of having ghost classes haunting your code base is that it can provoke fear of making changes because of what might happen from unknown objects that pop up at the wrong moment.

What is the root cause?
Poltergeist objects and classes, which can be called **ghosts**, are the result of good intentions going bad. Often, their classes were implemented to solve a temporary architectural issue, but the programmer never had the chance to complete their design, and thus you end up with objects in memory that are present, but their reason for being is not apparent.

How to avoid this?
Here are some tips that might help you avoid this anti-pattern:

- Don't use design patterns that you don't fully understand
- Schedule weekly code-base reviews and remove deprecated code
- Use source-control branching strategies to manage the refactoring of significant components
- Add TODO comments in your code and ask your team to review them and take action regularly
- Write the documentation before implementing a new architecture so that your team can review your plan and give you feedback before you make changes

> Being a minimalist is a good mindset for a programmer. Code can be complicated, but it should never be bloated with things that are useless. Focus always on what is essential and remove what is not.

Premature optimization

"Perfection is attained by slow degrees; it requires the hand of time."

- Voltaire

What is it?
Premature optimization is the act of optimizing and perfecting your code before it's needed and, as a result, wasting precious production time.

Why is it wrong?
Investing more time than needed on optimization is one of the worst ways to waste your time and that of your employer. Most devices are getting faster every year, and, thus, programmers are less required to optimize their code to run faster on limited hardware.

What is the root cause?
A lack of experience is usually the root cause.

How to avoid this?
Always profile your code before optimizing it. For those who might not know, **profiling** is the act of using diagnostic tools that help you analyze the performance of your system. Often, you will discover that the performance bottlenecks in your code are limited to specific areas in your source code, so by focusing on those, you can gain speed without having to refactor your entire code base.

Like a good mechanic, a programmer should have a toolbox filled with tools that can help them work faster and better.

Vendor lock-in

"It's not a faith in technology. It's faith in people."

- Steve Jobs

What is it?
Vendor lock-in happens when you start integrating third-party components, plugins, frameworks, or libraries in your code base, but become dependent on them to make your code function properly.

Why is it wrong?
In the context of a Unity project, being dependent on third-party libraries can limit your ability to upgrade to a new version of Unity because you might need to wait for patches from the vendor in order to avoid going backward.

What is the root cause?
Buying Plug and Play components and libraries from third-party vendors saves a lot of production time, so it's very tempting to use them to a point where you become too dependent on them.

How to avoid this?
You should research a vendor before buying their products and integrating them into your code base. For example, if they are not updating their support forums, it might be an indication that they are not planning to release updates shortly, and this might limit your capacity to get immediate support if required.

As a Unity developer, you should always check the Unity Asset store before writing anything because there's probably someone who has already done what you want to do, but in a better way.

Management by numbers

What is it?

Managing by numbers is the tendency to take management decisions based heavily on statistics that are generated by tools, such as Excel spreadsheets or reports, rather than on an accurate analysis of what is going on in a project.

Why is it wrong?

Numbers expressed in productivity reports often don't mirror the quality or the potential of a team. They can hide issues that are provoked by dynamic human interactions, instead of exposing them. This focus on numbers can blind project managers during critical decision-making processes. In other words, can you define the level of productivity of a programmer by the amount of bugs they fix in a week? The answer is *no*, because the complexity of a particular bug is not a constant. You can't evaluate a programmer who fixes five simple bugs in a week the same way as another programmer who resolves a single but very complex one in the same period.

What is the root cause?

Numbers are easy to explain and justify, especially when communicating with higher management that doesn't have the technical expertise to evaluate a project beyond very general indicators. This approach can result in an organization that spends its time focusing on figures instead of actual results.

How to avoid this?

Senior programmers should challenge project managers who are using general statistics and numbers to evaluate the progress of a project by offering more concrete indicators of quality and improvement. Here is an example:

- Update versus downtime of services
- The rate of bugs found and fixed over time

Probably the most critical thing you can do to guarantee yourself a long career in the tech industry after you hit 40 is to go back to school and get a diploma or certification in management. This type of education will permit you to transition into a long-term leadership role, which companies will probably encourage you to consider after you have attained several decades of experience.

The technical interview

"I choose a lazy person to do a hard job. Because a lazy person will find an easy way to do it."

-Bill Gates

What is it?
The concept of a technical interview in the hiring process of a programmer might not sound like an anti-pattern in itself, but I'm proposing that it is, and one that has side-effects in the quality of source code produced by a team. For those who have never experienced a programmer technical interview, it involves a series of tests that are given to the candidate to validate their skills and knowledge. The exams may include writing answers about programming on a whiteboard, a piece of paper, or in an online test environment. I consider the technical interview an industry-wide anti-pattern.

Why is it wrong?
The core issue of the technical interview process is that you can only test for what you already know. Thus, you will end up recruiting candidates who are mirror images of yourself. As a result, you will end up building a team that lacks a range of different skills. This approach is valid if your only goal is to have a very specialized team, but this is a rare case. Most companies need to have employees with varied skillsets to balance out any weaknesses in the organization.

For example, if your subject of focus of your technical interview revolves around data structures because this is your strength as the interviewer, then you might end up eliminating candidates who are weaker in that area but stronger in other areas, such as design patterns. But because you are evaluating only on what you consider to be important, based on your technical bias, you might miss out on hiring candidates who could bring new skills to your team.

What is the root cause?

The main reason why the hiring process of programmers is so inconsistent throughout our industry is that few people understand what programmers do and how to evaluate them as candidates. So, hiring managers prefer to judge applicants by their final technical test scores, thereby reducing the value of a candidate to a single number.

There are also some types of interviewer behavior patterns or processes that may also be part of the root cause:

- **The Riddler**: A riddler is an interviewer who wants to test the skills of a candidate by asking questions in the form of clever puzzles. This approach often ends up confusing most candidates and turning the interview process into a stressful game.
- **The Hot Seat**: The infamous hot seat interview type is similar to a police interrogation with the goal of isolating a candidate's weaknesses and strengths with a rapid succession of questions. Often, one interviewer will take the role of the *bad cop* by being more aggressive in their questioning, while another plays the *good cop* to assist the candidate if they take too long to answer some questions. This approach ends up burning out the candidate or forcing them to answer in a way that they think is what the interviewers want to hear. This is not a suitable method to learn about the potential of a candidate.
- **The Whiteboard**: The whiteboard interview consists of having the candidate answer technical questions by writing their answer on a whiteboard. There's a particular issue with this method of evaluating candidates; most programmers never write code on paper or whiteboards during their career, so when forced to do so during a stressful situation such as an interview will result in a lot of false negatives about their actual skill level.

How to avoid this?

Almost everyone agrees that hiring good programmers is a costly and challenging process, but this means that you need to be more creative in the way you approach technical interviews, so you don't end up rejecting excellent candidates for ones who are just clones of who you already have in your team.

Here are some tips that can help you avoid this anti-pattern:

- Try to see what is unique and valuable in a candidate. Get a candidate who can teach you and your team something new.
- Don't probe for weaknesses. Instead, try to understand a candidate's strengths and see whether they balance with their potential weaknesses.

- Always take into consideration the fact that there's a variety of skills that a programmer might have in the industry, depending on their specialization. For example, the average web developer might not be as strong at math as a 3D programmer, but they might be better at normalizing databases or designing client-server applications.
- When a candidate fails to answer a technical question, ask yourself whether this is because they don't understand it, might not have the skills to do so, or might be too nervous because of the examination process. In other words, the context of the interview is important, not just the final score, when evaluating the actual skill level of an applicant.

Even if you are a very experienced professional programmer, you should never underestimate the potential difficulty of a modern-day technical interview process. Your years of experience might be a disadvantage because interviewers usually want to evaluate whether you still know your computer science basics. In other words, you might have to answer questions about subjects that you might not have reviewed since university. So it's a good idea to dust off those old school books and study the basics before going into an interview.

Summary

We have arrived at the end of our journey. Throughout this book, we explored various design patterns, each with their unique abilities. The most important takeaway from this book is that before you start writing a single line of code, you should always verify whether there's a pattern that matches the design intention of a system before building it. This approach avoids reinventing the wheel and offers you a consistent methodology to programming that will help you throughout your career.

But this chapter also exposes that what looks like a valid design or management decision can quickly go wrong without awareness of the motivations and potential consequences behind it. In other words, as programmers, we need to be mindful of the potential implications of our decisions, at every level, or we can fall victim to Anti-Patterns.

Exercise

For our final exercise, I'm making you a list of daily habits that will ensure a long and prosperous career as a programmer in the game industry. However, a failure to enhance your skills gradually will almost guarantee that you will end up getting stuck in mediocrity and possibly irrelevance. Trust me; it happened to me until, one day, I decided to change my habits and focus again on gaining true mastery over my craft.

Here are some good habits to form:

- Learn at least one new programming language per year.
- Check your skills regularly by taking practice-interview programming exams.
- Attain a new technical certification every year, such as the PMP, CCNA, and CEH.
- Make a list of all your weaknesses as a programmer and work on them every day.
- Try to attend at least one technology-related meet-up event or conference per week.
- Join technical professional organizations, such as ACM and IEEE, and use the resources on offer.
- Keep yourself up to date in terms of what's happening by reading tech and game industry news every day.
- Take courses on subjects from other fields that might be related to yours, including management, UI design, and animation.
- Make yourself a list of blogs and YouTube channels that are related to technology and programming. Read at least one blog post and watch a video per day.
- Attend a coding bootcamp or subscribe to at least one training program per month. Don't forget to complete them.
- Read at least two books about programming or related fields per year.
- Open a GitHub account and contribute to at least one open source project, even if it's just a couple of lines of code. Get used to the process and the community.
- Learn meditation; it's a stressful job; knowing how to stay calm under pressure will help you maintain your mental health and avoid burning out.

For our final exercise, I would recommend that you make a list of your favorite patterns and ask yourself why you like them. Is it because they're easy to implement, or because they resolve actual architectural issues in your code? In other words, make sure that you don't use a specific pattern for the wrong reasons, never be lazy, and always be conscious with your choices when writing code.

Further reading

Organizations:

- *ACM*
  `https://www.acm.org`
- *IEEE*
  `https://www.ieee.org`

Blogs:

- *Coding Horror*
  `https://blog.codinghorror.com`
- *Joel on Software*
  `https://www.joelonsoftware.com`
- *Scott Hanselman Blog*
  `https://www.hanselman.com/blog/`
- *The Crazy Programmer*
  `https://www.thecrazyprogrammer.com`

YouTube:

- *Computerphile*
  `https://www.youtube.com/user/Computerphile`
- *Success in Tech*
  `https://www.youtube.com/channel/UC-vYrOAmtrx9sBzJAf3x_xw`
- *TED*
  `https://www.youtube.com/user/TEDtalksDirector`
- *TechLead*
  `https://www.youtube.com/channel/UC4xKdmAXFh4ACyhpiQ_3qBw`

Tech news:

- *Slashdot*
  `https://slashdot.org`
- *Wired*
  `https://www.wired.com`
- *Gamasutra*
  `http://www.gamasutra.com`
- GamesIndustry.biz
  `https://www.gamesindustry.biz`

Online courses:

- *Udemy*
  `https://www.udemy.com`
- *Lynda*
  `https://www.lynda.com`
- *Pluralsight*
  `https://www.pluralsight.com`
- MasterClass
  `https://www.masterclass.com`

Books:

- *Anti-patterns: Managing Software Organizations and People,* by Colin J. Neill, Philip A. Laplante, and Joanna F. DeFranco
  `https://www.crcpress.com/Antipatterns-Managing-Software-Organizations-and-People-Second-Edition/Neill-Laplante-DeFranco/p/book/9781439861868`

Other Books You May Enjoy

If you enjoyed this book, you may be interested in these other books by Packt:

Unity 2018 Cookbook - Third Edition
Matt Smith

ISBN: 9781788471909

- Get creative with Unity's shaders and learn to build your own shaders with the new Shader Graph tool
- Create a text and image character dialog with the free Fungus Unity plugin
- Explore new features integrated into Unity 2018, including TextMesh Pro and ProBuilder
- Master Unity audio, including ducking, reverbing, and matching pitch to animation speeds
- Work with the new Cinemachine and timeline to intelligently control camera movements
- Improve ambiance through the use of lights and effects, including reflection and light probes
- Create stylish user interfaces with the UI system, including power bars and clock displays

Unity Virtual Reality Projects - Second Edition
Jonathan Linowes

ISBN: 9781788478809

- Create 3D scenes with Unity and other 3D tools while learning about world space and scale
- Build and run VR applications for specific headsets, including Oculus, Vive, and Daydream
- Interact with virtual objects using eye gaze, hand controllers, and user input events
- Move around your VR scenes using locomotion and teleportation
- Implement an audio fireball game using physics and particle systems
- Implement an art gallery tour with teleportation and data info
- Design and build a VR storytelling animation with a soundtrack and timelines
- Create social VR experiences with Unity networking

Leave a review - let other readers know what you think

Please share your thoughts on this book with others by leaving a review on the site that you bought it from. If you purchased the book from Amazon, please leave us an honest review on this book's Amazon page. This is vital so that other potential readers can see and use your unbiased opinion to make purchasing decisions, we can understand what our customers think about our products, and our authors can see your feedback on the title that they have worked with Packt to create. It will only take a few minutes of your time, but is valuable to other potential customers, our authors, and Packt. Thank you!

Index

Printed in Great Britain
by Amazon